Race and Ethnicity

Concepts in the Social Sciences

Series Editor: Frank Parkin

Published Titles

Race and Ethnicity
John Rex

OPEN UNIVERSITY PRESS
Milton Keynes

Open University Press
12 Cofferidge Close
Stony Stratford
Milton Keynes MK11 1BY, England

First published 1986
Reprinted 1989

British Library Cataloguing in Publication Data

Rex, John
  Race and ethnicity—(Concepts in the
  social sciences)
  1. Race relations
  I. Title   II. Series
  305.8   HT1521

  ISBN 0 335 15386 0
  ISBN 0 335 15385 2 Pbk

Text designed by Clarke Williams

Typeset by Mathematical Composition Setters Ltd, Salisbury, UK
Printed in Great Britain by
St Edmundsbury Press Ltd, Bury St Edmunds, Suffolk

Contents

Preface

This book was written during a partly sabbatical year at St. Catherine's College, Oxford while the Research Unit on Ethnic Relations of which I had been Director was transferred from Birmingham to the University of Warwick as a Designated Economic and Social Research Council Centre.

The Research Unit on Ethnic Relations was originally set up in Bristol in the early seventies and was moved under my direction to the University of Aston in Birmingham in 1979. Its remit at the time of my appointment was to pursue fundamental research in the area of race and ethnic relations. Shortly after I joined, however, the Social Science Research Council became concerned that the work of its Units and Centres should be policy-relevant and they were urged more and more to address themselves to policy questions.

It was by no means easy for our Unit to satisfy all the conflicting demands made upon us. Its area of research was politically sensitive and Black and other Ethnic Minority Organizations were profoundly suspicious of any organization set up and backed ultimately by government. The Unit had tried to maintain its independence both in relation to government pressure and in relation to the rhetoric of political organizations, and it was essential that it should be clear about the central theoretical questions. From 1980 onwards this had to be done by a Unit which was also called upon to deal with policy questions.

Fortunately all the Units underwent a further change of status in 1984 when they were converted into Designated Research Centres which were part of universities. The Research Unit on Ethnic Relations became the Centre for Research in Ethnic Relations at the

University of Warwick. Professor Robin Cohen of that University took over executive responsibility for the management of its programme and I was given a sabbatical year to bring together some of the theoretical themes that had informed our work.

I am very grateful indeed to Dr Ceri Peach and the Master and Fellows of St Catherine's College, Oxford for providing me with an excellent academic home while I wrote this book. Especially, too, I should like to thank Audrey Hiscock and Susan Seville who showed great patience in typing my manuscript. My thanks are also obviously due to Professor Robin Cohen and my colleagues at the Centre, whose past and present empirical work has helped to shape my theoretical ideas.

John Rex
Centre for Research in Ethnic Relations
University of Warwick
August 1985

Chapter 1

Sociological Concepts and The Field of Ethnic and Race Relations

This book deals with what is obviously one of the more important topics in the political sociology of the modern world, but, unfortunately, one which plays too little part in the current theorizations of the sociologists. Either they seem to describe an idealized world in which conflicts hardly exist (as in the so-called structural-functionalism of Talcott Parsons, 1951) or they see these conflicts as arising almost entirely from a basis in class structure. It is not my intention to dispute the importance of class conflict or even to deny that there is some value in devising an ideal type of a world without conflicts: indeed I shall argue that there are close similarities and a strong relationship between class conflict and race and ethnic conflict, and something of what I have to say may be interpreted as dealing with the problem of order in colonial, post-colonial and metropolitan societies. Nonetheless, a sociology which fails to account for the specific racial and ethnic element in political conflict is of little use in providing a sociological approach to the actual problems of the modern world.

Styles of Conceptualization in Sociology

The study of ethnic and race relations is concerned with the kinds of social relations which exist between people of the same race and ethnicity and between individuals or groups of different race and ethnicity. It does belong, therefore, within the field of sociology. Unfortunately, however, sociology is beset by conflicts and disagreements; not merely about paradigms in general, but about the very categories in terms of which concepts are elaborated. It is necessary, therefore, at the outset of this study to consider some of the options open to the sociology of race and ethnic relations in terms of the style of its conceptualization, then, having made a choice, to outline some of the basic concepts to which the study of race and ethnic relations has to be related.

The issues involved here have been raised in a sharp form by the startling claims made on behalf of what is called 'rational choice theory': that there is one and only one scientific approach to the study of race relations (Hechter 1983, Banton 1983, Mason and Rex 1986). Hechter argues that the theory of rational choice must be adopted because of the proven inadequacies of certain other theories, of which he discusses 'normativism' and the theory of constraint. Banton rejects the notion that racially and ethnically oriented behaviour is explicable, whether in terms of external constraints or constraints of the personality system taking the form of prejudice. Both claim to be 'methodological individualists' and also that rational choice theory uniquely embodies the methodological individualist approach. (Methodological Individualism involves in some sense the notion that social structures are to be explained and analyzed in terms of the actions and expectations of individuals. Rational Choice Theory expressed most clearly in economic theory involves the assumption that individual action is determined by value preferences of individual actions.) Of course neither Hechter nor Banton suggests that behaviour is solely the product of rational choice, but that, given the existing constraints, behaviour can be predicted only if the schedule of the actor's preferences is also known.

The range of alternatives posed by the rational choice theorists, therefore, seems to include that which emphasizes constraint and may be traced back to Durkheim (1938), that which emphasizes norms and was at the heart of the immensely influential sociology of Talcott Parsons (1951), and that which is based on the concept of prejudice which, as a result of the work of the Authoritarian Personality school, (Adorno *et al.* 1950), played a large part in shaping the study of race and ethnic relations in post-war America. If none of these are adequate as theories, it is argued, then the only remaining alternative is rational choice theory, based upon the methodological individualist approach. In opposition to this I shall argue that there is another alternative, deriving especially from the work of Weber and the early Marx and not based on 'constraint', 'normativism' or 'prejudice', and that it can claim to represent a more serious application of the tenets of methodological individualism.

The 'constraint' approach is clearly based upon the methodology of Emile Durkheim and his injunction to the sociologist to treat social facts as 'things'. This involves a tendency towards determinism and even fatalism. It also ignores the problems about the nature of social science raised by the neo-Kantian school, which always recognized that the study of human action could not be adequately pursued using the categories of natural science (Rex 1985). Hechter, however, is right in suggesting that this has been a dominant approach in sociological work, including his own (Mason and Rex 1986), which draws on statistical evidence to suggest casual relationships. I share Hechter's belief in the inadequacy of such work, but on the more fundamental ground that such statistics do not represent 'things', but rather the actions of other individuals. As I once put it: 'The paradox of sociology lies precisely in this: that that which appears to constrain us from outside is in fact the product of human action and can be changed by human action' (Rex 1973).

The 'normative' approach is strongly associated with 'systems-theory' in the work of Talcott Parsons (1937 and 1952). According to him, the study of human society in a scientific way cannot be based upon the notion of means-ends rationality with the ends of action being 'random' from the point of view of the system (Parsons 1937, p. 66). The study of actual societies suggests to him that the choice of means is not purely rational, but is governed by the application of norms which cannot be said to be rational or irrational, and that the ends which men seek, in at least an important part of their action, are not random but contribute to the maintenance of the system. In this way Parsons suggests that the problem of the 'order' which is evident in human society is solved. Men may act in terms of means-ends rationality but it is within a framework that involves the normative determination both of the ends sought and the means used. I would say this approach is useful as an ideal type, but if sociology is to be at all applicable to the real world it must supplement normative theories with conflict theory which posits conflicting ends being sought by different actors and the rational pursuit of those ends by appropriate means.

One useful suggestion made by Parsons in an earlier work (Parsons, Shils *et al*. 1962) is that the understanding of action may involve reference to three systems: the culture system, the social system and the personality system. The social system, with which he chose to deal, took account of the constraints of the other two systems, but also had its own dynamic. Thus the norms which influenced human action were affected by their systemic relations with other aspects of culture, and the personality system placed some constraints upon what the individual could be socialized into accepting as appropriate to his action. In other words men were affected in their behaviour by the norms of their society and by relatively rigid psychological dispositions often called prejudices (Parsons speaks of compulsive action).

However much Parsons may have recognized the culture system and the personality system, he certainly did not accept that either of these systems completely determined social action. The social system based upon the interaction of one individual with another had its own dynamic and its own laws. The individual was constrained not merely by his personality or by his inherited culture but by the contingencies of interaction with others. This is certainly the position which I take here. I would recognize both that action in the interracial and intercultural sphere may be *influenced* by the rigidities and constraints of personality and that it might also in part be the result of inherited cultural norms, but this by no means involves accepting that the whole of such action can be explained in this way. In particular, the sociology of race and culture relations has to take account of the often conflicting goals of individual and group actions and the power which can be deployed in support of different goals.

This leads us to the kind of sociology which will characterize this volume. Like rational choice theory, it takes its stand on the side of methodological individualism. It does not introduce the notion of collective entities as 'things' which 'cause' behaviour, but places emphasis upon human action. What differentiates it from rational choice theory, however, is recognition that the action of any one individual is constrained by the action or the potentiality for action of others.

There are versions of rational choice theory which take account of the behaviour of other actors than ego, but they are usually based upon exchange theory which assumes that ego and alter are able to strike happy bargains to their mutual advantage. Hechter (Mason and Rex 1986) even goes further in recognizing in Marx an account of the congealed actions of others which is 'alienating' to ego. But there is no clear conceptual account in any of these theories of the structures in terms of which alter's actions comes into conflict with that of ego.

No such account is available, of course, within the economistic and utilitarian type of theory which has led to the attempt to widen the scope of the theory of rational choice. But it is available in the neo-Kantian tradition and especially in the work of Max Weber. The conceptualization of the field which will be suggested here draws heavily upon his work.

The central important notion in the theoretical writing of Max Weber is that groups and structures of social relations are not to be understood as socially constraining things. They are the actions and probabilities of action of other individuals. As Weber puts it in defining a 'social relationship':

> The term 'social relationship' will be used to denote the behaviour of a plurality of actors insofar as, in its meaningful content, the action of each takes account of that of others and is oriented in these terms. The social relationship thus consists entirely and exclusively in the existence of a probability that there will be a meaningful course of social action ...
>
> (Weber 1968, Vol. 1, p. 26)

Constraint within social relations therefore is not a constraint by things but by a probability of action. Such probabilities can be resisted and changed. Alternatively, one might say that the question of whether ego's goals, or those of alter whose actions act as a constraint on him is a value question. In saying that such-and-such *must* be the case we are in effect taking sides.

There is a close similarity between Weber and the early Marx on this point. For Marx the decisive category is that of 'sensuous human activity'. The human essence is said to be 'the ensemble of social relations', but this ensemble may be 'understood in its contradictions and revolutionized in practice' (Marx 1957).

Clearly the adoption of this perspective is of the first importance for the study of race or ethnic relations. It does not permit the conclusion that if a member of a racial or ethnic group RE is confronted by the demands of another racial or ethnic group RE_a, it must comply. Nor does it accept that the group RE *must* bargain and arrive at terms of exchange, even though it recognizes this as one possibility. It leaves open the possibility that RE may mobilize sanctions of resistance to change RE_a's demand or likely behaviour.

There is, however, a danger of utopianism if this perspective is applied to ethnic groups, just as there is a danger if it is applied to individuals. Social reality is in fact often intransigent and it may only be possible to change the behaviour of RE_a by changing the behaviour of RE_b which is a constraint upon RE_a, and so on, in long chains of interconnected relationships. A realistic sociology of race and ethnic relations, like a realistic sociology of anything else, requires the recognition of these claims. Weber, indeed, took this so seriously in his general philosophy of history that he ultimately saw ego as confronted by a vast bureaucratized world in which he himself became little more than a cog in a vast machine (Weber 1930).

There is nonetheless a world of difference between saying that external constraints are things and saying that we are caught up in chains of social relationships. The latter are in principle subject to change and are the responsibility of human beings. For this reason Weber insisted that group concepts or structural concepts of any kind should be capable of being unpacked in terms of the actions and expectations of individuals. The Marx of the Thesis on Feverbach believed this too. While the 'secret of the Holy Family' (i.e. social relations and ideas in the ideological superstructure) was to be found in 'the earthy family', this latter, and through the latter, the former, could in fact be understood and changed.

It would seem possible in principle, therefore, to develop a style of sociology which does justice both to methodological individualism and to conflict theory, and that a theory of this kind is far more relevant to the sociology of race and ethnic relations than one which fatalistically accepts the status quo or which imagines that a free market of exchanges is capable of achieving interracial or interethnic harmony.

However, methodologically individualist and conflict-oriented sociology has to respond to another challenge, one which is imposed by 'structuralism'. Thus it is sometimes claimed that there are patterns in social life which are relatively unmalleable to which ego is bound to subordinate his action. It is suggested that methodological individualism with its small-scale models of interaction between hypothetical individuals is not really capable of dealing with these patterns or structures.

Now there is some truth in this. Weber himself recognizes that

> concepts of collective entities which are found both in common sense and in juristic or other technical forms of thought, have a meaning in the minds of individual persons, partly as something actually existing, partly as something having normative authority. This is true not only of judges and officials, but of ordinary private individuals as well. Actors thus in part orient their action to them and in this role such ideas have a powerful, often a decisive casual influence on the course of action of real individuals.
>
> (Weber 1968, Vol. 1 p. 14)

To take a simple example, in the study of kinship, the social anthropologist seeking to understand ego's behaviour vis-à-vis different members of his kin may refer to certain principles, such as the principle of the unity of the sibling group or the unity of the lineage, to explain why apparently different relatives receive the same treatment. This involves an extension of the notion of ego having expectations of specific others through the introduction into one explanatory model of intellectual principles which are imputed to ego.

If this is true even in the relatively simple case of kinship systems, it is of course much more true in the case of large-scale political and economic structures, and one must assume that individuals in planning their action do take account of such structures. It is important, therefore, that the sociologist should seek to understand the 'principles' in terms of which such structures work. What is called structuralism might be seen as an attempt to elucidate such principles. It might be added, moreover, that Weber is a structuralist in this sense, having devoted the substantive chapters of his *Economy and Society* to elucidating the principles according to which economic, political, legal, religious and urban structures worked.

But even here it should be noted that such structures are not to be thought of as things. They have explanatory significance because not only the theoretical sociologist but the participant actor ego is able to understand them. Alfred Schutz commenting on Weber's work suggested that it was governed by what he called the 'postulate of adequacy'. Thus

> Each term in a scientific model of human action must be constructed in such a way that a human act performed within a lifeworld by an individual actor in the way indicated by the typical construct would be understandable by the actor himself as well as for his fellow man in terms of common-sense interpretation of everyday life. Compliance with the postulate warrants consistency of the constructs of the sociologist with the constructs of common-sense experience of social reality.
>
> (Schutz 1967)

For the study undertaken here, it means that we should not be looking for abstract structural principles relating to race and ethnic relations which a participant actor could not understand, but that we should seek to understand systems of race and ethnic relations in a way which in principle the participants themselves can understand.

The recognition of structural principles, as governing the behaviour of ego and alter, moreover, does not exclude the possibility of conflict. Ego may recognize a world in which he wishes to see certain principles operating in the organization of patterns of social relations, but he may also recognize that in the world as it actually is and in the mind of alter, other principles operate or are thought to be desirable. Our models should then recognize the possibility that principle might be set against principle and that the total structure is liable to change.

Having identified my theoretical position as one which is based upon methodological individualism but which recognizes the possibility of conflict, I must now go beyond the style of conceptualization to the development of actual structural concepts which might be useful in the analysis of race and ethnic relations. The key question here is to what extent do such relations turn on the formation of 'groups' and the interaction between groups. The sociology of race and ethnic relations has always had difficulty dealing with this question, and it is desirable to begin with the general question of what is meant by a 'group' and what other structures of social relations there might be. Again it is useful to do this with the aid of Max Weber.

The Group and other Structures of Social Relations

Weber actually fails to give a definition of a group as such. He does, however, distinguish between social relationships which are open and those which are closed. As he puts it:

> A social relationship . . . . will be spoken of as 'open' to outsiders if and insofar as its system of order does not deny participation to anyone who wishes to join and is in a position to do so. A relationship will, on the other hand, be called 'closed' against outsiders so far as according to its subjective meaning and boundary rules, participation of certain persons is excluded, limited or subject to conditions.
>
> (Weber 1968, Vol. 1 p. 43)

The first characteristic I have in mind when I speak of a group, then, involves a closed social relationship. This, however, is not the only characteristic of a group. A second such characteristic is the imputation to individual actors of representativeness and responsibility. Weber defines the terms 'representative' and 'responsibility' as follows:

> Within a social relationship, whether it is traditional or enacted, certain kinds of action of each participant may be imputed to all others in which case we speak of mutually responsible members; or

the action of certain members may imputed to the others (the 'represented').

(Weber 1968, Vol. 1 p. 46)

The notions of representativeness and responsibility within closed social relationships are important because together they make collective social action possible. A social relationship *as such* cannot act, but when the parties to it may be held responsible amongst themselves both *to* themselves and to outsiders, and when one party may be thought of as a representative, it is possible to conceive of collective action. This is particularly important to us here because what is loosely called an ethnic group does *not* have the characteristic that its members accept responsibility and recognize representatives, even though such imputations may be made by outsiders.

As I see it, a further though not essential aspect of a group is that it recognizes a head or leader. Weber calls a groups of this type a '*verband*', which Roth and Wittich translate as 'organisation'. As Weber says:

A social relationship which is closed or limits the admission of outsiders will be called an organization when its regulations are enforced by specific individuals; a chief and, possibly an administrative staff which normally has representative powers.

(Weber 1968, Vol. 1 p. 48)

All social relationships, and not merely the closed variety, may be either communal or associative. According to Weber:

A social relationship will be called 'communal' if and insofar as the orientation to social action ... is based upon the subjective feeling of the parties whether affectual or traditional that they belong together.

A social relationship will be called 'associative' if and insofar as the orientation of action within it rests upon a rationally motivated adjustment of interests or a similarly motivated agreement, whether the basis of the rational judgement be absolute values or reasons of expediency.

(ibid. p. 40)

Obviously there follows the possibility that communal social relations may be closed and may come to have the characteristics of a group. Where both these conditions are fulfilled we may refer to a community. Another possibility, however, is that, though social relations are communal and closed, they may not have the characteristics of a group and are not therefore communities. What are loosely called 'ethnic groups' come under this heading. They

are not themselves groups or communities, but groups and communities may be formed by some of their members.

This notion of a collectivity amid a network of social relationships of a communal kind, which is not of itself a group but which
could give rise to group formation, is essential to this study. It is
also relevant to the study of classes, status groups and nations
without states (e.g. the Basques). For lack of a better term, I will
refer to such sociological entities as quasi-groups. Edna Bonacich
(1980) here suggests the term 'communalities'. This is a useful
innovation but there is perhaps the danger that it may not be
distinguished from 'communities'.

Under this heading, one should finally notice that the distinctions
between communal and associative relations and between communities and associations are not absolute. A community may set
up procedures to attain specific ends in a relatively rational,
calculating way, and by acting together the members of an association may come to feel that they belong together. Ethnic quasi-
groups and ethnic communities may generate group action of an
associative type. On the other hand, though classes tend to express
themselves in the form of associations based upon a rational
adjustment of interest, they may also come to have communal
characteristics.

Concepts of Class and Status

Since we are concerned with the interaction of large scale collectivities or quasi-groups, sociological terminology which refers to
class, status and similar terms is of particular interest to us. I avoid
using the term 'stratification' here, popular though it is amongst
sociologists, because I want to make it clear that I do not accept
the notion of inert strata which the geological metaphor implicit in
this term suggests. In any case, I shall be considering whether
ethnic and racial quasi-groups are similar in structure, overlap
with, or are even the product of, class and status formations.

In Weber's way of thinking, what he calls 'class situation' is
dependent upon market situation, therefore to understand the use
of the term class we must first define what we mean by a market.

A market involves two types of relationships: bargaining and
exchange, and competition. Under bargaining and exchange, we
assume that the parties own or control different goods and services
and will make them available to others only insofar as the others
provide goods and services not previously owned or controlled. The
exact quantity of goods and services offered or required will be

settled when the parties have calculated the cost of giving away that previously controlled and the benefit of gaining access to that which is not controlled. It is, of course, possible that agreement on these costs and benefits will be reached amicably as exchange theory (Homans 1961, Balu 1964) and rational choice theory (Banton 1983, p.109) suggest. But it is also possible that the parties will deploy more radical sanctions to force one another to accept particular terms.

Sanctions used in exchange relationships may be of many kinds. As the old couplet has it, the parties may take the view that there should be a resort to force,

> The mountain sheep are sweeter, but the valley sheep are fatter
> We therefore deemed it meeter, to swallow up the latter

but there is a whole gradation of possible sanctions of a more or less violent, more or less peaceful kind. The most peaceful, other than the appeal to some moral principle, is the threat to go to a supplier who can offer a better rate of exchange or better terms. A free market situation is one in which exchanges take place on terms which are determined after taking into account the possible amounts of goods and services offered by the supplier's competitor.

As Weber sees it, a market situation will arise wherever there is a differential distribution of property, and these market situations will lead to class situations. These may differ according to the kind of property and the kind of services being offered. *Inter alia* Weber mentions

> Ownership of dwellings; workshops; warehouses; stores; agriculturally usable land in large and small holdings; .... ownership of mines; cattle; men; slaves; disposition over mobile instruments of production; of capital goods of all sorts, especially money or objects that can be exchanged for money; disposition over products of one's labour or others' labour ...; dispositions over transferable monopolies of any kind.
>
> (Weber 1968, p. 927)

Thus for Weber there are many possible markets and a multiplicity of class situations. A class is simply a number of individuals who share any market situation.

Marx, of course, confined the term class specifically to situations arising in the labour market. He was also much more pessimistic than Weber about this market situation and the class conflict to which it gives rise being peacefully resolved.

My own view is that while class situations do not arise solely in the labour market as Marx suggests, the markets on which they rest are inherently unstable and market bargaining frequently gives way to more drastic forms of conflict. I would suggest that the possibility of using the sanction of going to another supplier is frequently eliminated by the development of monopolies on both sides. Two parties then confront one another for collective bargaining. Though they may peacefully settle on a price after taking account of the costs and benefits of having and not having particular quantities of certain goods and services, they will frequently resort to non-economic sanctions. In the labour market these may at first be confined to the strike and the lock-out, and in other markets to the boycott, but very often the parties will seek to use political sanctions either in the form of legitimate state power or in the form of overt violence.

In all societies, then, I am suggesting there are relatively unstable structures called markets and in the most important of these men unite in collectivities called classes to pursue shared interests.

Such classes are not groups or organizations and it may be said they are based in the first place on associative relations, i.e. in Weber's terms 'on a rational adjustment of interests'. They may, however, give rise to groups and organizations, and produce in class members a communal feeling of belonging together. It should be obvious therefore that classes have sociological characteristics very similar to those of ethnic quasi-groups.

Of the first importance of this study is a theoretical possibility that ethnic quasi-groups will enter into a market relationship with each other. They will then have some of the characteristics of classes, with the additional feature that they already possess a feeling of belonging together, which classes based upon a rational adjustment of interest only gradually acquire. On the other hand, as a class organizes itself for political action, it may well draw upon ethnic feelings of belonging together amongst its members as a means of binding members more closely together.

Markets are one of the bases for the formation of groups. But they are not the only one. In many societies, the most important inequalities arise not because of the differential distribution of property, but because of differences of legal and political rights. When this is the case we speak of estates rather than classes. They are exemplified by the social system of Medieval Europe, but they are also crucial in the construction of colonial societies following Europe's expansion overseas.

While the basis of estates lies in the inequality of access to legal protection and to political power, they very quickly acquire the additional characteristic of being closed social groups with a distinctive style of life, adherence or non-adherence to which becomes the basis of closure. An estate comes to constitute itself as community in which the consciousness of kind generated by the possession of a shared culture binds members closely together. Estates are also organized in systems of higher and lower estates. The higher estates claim a greater degree of esteem or honour than the lower ones, and so long as the system remains stable, they succeed in getting this claim recognized by those beneath them.

Estates systems in Europe arose partly from conquest but also by natural social differentiation between those who bore arms and those whose task was to provide food for the soldiers. In the colonial case the act of conquest was much more central, and ethnic-quasi groups were often 'differentially incorporated' into the society, that is to say they had differing degrees of political power and access to legal protection from their conquerors.

One particular variant of an estate system is the traditional caste system of India. In addition to the general characteristics of an estate system it is also marked by a strong connection between the estate and occupational specialization, a high degree of religious rationalization and a high degree of consent to the system by the lower castes.

Estates disappear with the growth of democracy and the nation-state, in which in theory all individuals enjoy the same legal and political rights. Nonetheless 'status groups' still survive and it is to these rather than legal estates that Weber refers in his discussion of class, status and party. As he puts it:

> In contrast to classes, status groups (stande) are normally groups. They are however often of an amorphous kind. In contrast to the purely economically determined 'class situation' we wish to designate as 'status situation' every typical component of the life of men that is determined by a specific, positive or negative, social estimation of honour. The honour may be connected with any quality shared by a plurality and, of course, it can be knit to a class situation ...
>
> In content, status honour is normally expressed by the fact that above all else a specific style of life is expected from all those who wish to belong to the circle. Linked with these expectations are restrictions on social intercourse (that is intercourse which is not subservient to economic or any other purpose). These restrictions may confine normal marriages to within the status circle and may lead to complete endogenous closure.
>
> (Weber 1968, p. 932)

There is obviously some relationship between these closed groups practising a particular style of life and ethnic groups or quasi-groups (note that here Weber does suggest that status groups or stande are groups, but groups of an amorphous kind). There are, however, differences. Status groups as such are not hereditary, nor do their members necessarily even claim common descent. Ethnic groups or quasi-groups do. On the other hand, the relation between ethnic groups or quasi-groups is not necessarily one of hierarchy. Thus ethnicity and status may be thought of as independent variables. When they do come together and a shared way of life is coupled with the notion of shared descent, there is a movement, Weber believes, towards a caste system. This process is completed when the hereditary groups become attached to specific occupations.

If, however, status groups and ethnic groups are associated with caste, one may also ask what the relationship of each of these is to estate and class. Estates are clearly distinguished from castes and status groups by the fact that they involve legal and political differentiation, and classes by the fact that they are in conflict with one another. It may be suggested, however, that another tendency arising from status group formation is that, as it becomes subject to closure, it also seeks to monopolize political and legal privileges, thus becoming more like an estate. It is also the case that a status struggle which goes on between groups seeking to monopolize honour is very close to the notion of class bargaining and conflict.

So far as ethnic groups or quasi-groups are concerned, they may have features of status groups, estates and classes. They may be arranged in a hierarchy of honour, they may have different legal rights and they may have differential property rights. It would seem that while the sense of belonging together because of shared cultural characteristics and belief in a common ancestry brings men together in quasi-groups, the actual relations which arise between such quasi-groups may take a variety of forms, depending not on ethnicity itself, but upon other variable factors, including what characteristics are honoured, what legal rights are assigned to or obtained by the groups and what control they have over property. Because, moreover, participation in these other (status group, estate and class) systems actually serves to strengthen pre-existing ethnic bonds, it is not possible to study ethnicity realistically unless one sees its relationship to them.

One other type of status-ordering which we should also consider is that of an open-status system. Weber apparently thinks that, even in American society, status-situations move towards some type of closure and that what came to exist are status groups. The classical anthropological studies of W. Lloyd Warner and his col-leagues (Warner and Lunt 1947) seem to confirm this. But another possibility in open democratic societies is that styles of life may be open to all and that each individual is judged and accorded more or less honour and esteem according to the extent to which he attains such styles. This is what O.C. Cox (Cox 1970) rather perversely calls *social* class (contrasted with economic class) of which he says the basis is not structural but conceptual. No groups exist, only a series of reference points in terms of which men judge one another.

It does seem worthwhile retaining an ideal type of this kind in sociology, even though in practice there may be some tendency towards group formation or to closure in any empirical case. The question which then occurs is how ethnicity may be seen as related to status values of this kind. The answer is that the various ethnicities tend to be ordered conceptually in a hierarchy, and that the degree of a particular ethnicity is taken into account, along with other cultural characteristics, in assigning an individual to a place in the system. As the individual immigrant in American society advances up the status ladder, he becomes less ethnic (say Irish or Polish) at the same time as acquiring improved job, educational or housing characteristics.

Ethnic and Racial Groups as Such

Having discussed a number of the major ways in which the formation of groups and other structures of social relations occur, and having looked especially at the major forms of class and status relationship which occur within social systems and the relation of race and ethnicity to these, the question which now arises is whether race and ethnicity may be thought of as independent sources of action and social relations at all, or whether they are simply incidental to normal class and status processes.

Race as such cannot be thought of as causing action. The consensus of opinion amongst biologists appears to be (Hiernaux 1965) that although the world's populations can be classified in terms of a few physical characteristics—provided that it is recognized that even for these characteristics there is a considerable statistical spread and overlap—there is no evidence of mental characteristics being associated with these physical characteristics. Still less can race be thought of as having any relevance to the differential apportionment of rights amongst men.

But if race should not be thought of as a source or cause of action, it certainly can be an object of action orientation. Individuals may value physical characteristics similar to their own, identify with them and pursue actions with them so that they come to share not merely physical but cultural characteristics. At the same time those who do not share their characteristics may classify them with those who do and react to them as a category or group.

The basis of solidarity between members of a racial group is a matter of dispute. Some would deny it altogether, some would attribute it simply to a natural tendency towards what Giddings called 'consciousness of kind'. A more radical claim is that support for one's own is universal amongst human beings because of a genetically based tendency towards nepotism which itself survives because it maximizes the 'inclusive fitness' of those who have it. Race is a good marker of relatedness and it is natural that nepotism should be extended not merely to cousins and nephews but to more distant relatives whose relatedness is apparent from their shared physical characteristics.

Ethnic, as distinct from racial, attachment arises in several different ways. First, the culturally patterned forms of behaviour through which individuals satisfy their needs brings them into closer relations with some people than it does with others and they therefore find themselves part of a closed network. This is particularly true of actions in the private and domestic domain. Secondly, individuals may be drawn to others by the principle of 'consciousness of kind' operating through cultural as well as physical characteristics. Thirdly, it may be that similarity of cultural behaviour is taken as a sign of biological relatedness, and it is not surprising that those who share the same culture often claim to have a common ancestry.

In principle, physical and racial characteristics are less malleable than cultural characteristics and one would therefore expect ethnic groups or quasi-groups to be less stable than racial ones. Once it is recognized, however, that the physical characteristics do not determine membership of a racial group, but instead associated behaviour and attitudes towards physical characteristics, a racial group may be no more stable or unstable than an ethnic one. The notion of behaviour and group membership being determined by genetic inheritance is in any case false and can as easily be used to suggest a genetic basis for the behaviour of an ethnic group as it can for a racial one. In fact the most important distinction may not be between groups which have racial and cultural characteristics, but rather between those whose behavioural characteristics are held by others to have a genetic or other unalterable base. This in turn may depend upon the motivation of those who label the groups as racial or ethnic.

Here we are near to the heart of the problem of race and ethnic relations. This chapter has shown that there are many possible bases in the nature of group formation and in the development of class and status systems which serve to explain why human beings are driven to associate closely or to stay apart from and enter into conflict with others, quite apart from race and ethnicity. Differences of race and ethnicity give only a very slight basis in themselves for such alliances and conflicts. But since what are called racial and ethnic groups are groups (or quasi-groups) to whom common behavioural chacteristics are imputed, rather than groups which have such characteristics, it is clear that the creation of such groups may depend upon the non-racial non-ethnic context and the motivations to which it gives rise. The study of race relations is therefore inextricably tied up with the study of group formation generally and with the study of social class and status, or as many sociologists would say, of social stratification.

A corollary of this is that the distinction between racial and ethnic groups becomes problematic. These groups may be distinguished from each other by the actual physical and behavioural characteristics of members, but they may also be distinguished in terms of whether other people regard the basis of their behaviour as determined and unchangeable or undetermined and flexible. It is in fact common in political discussion to use the terms racial and ethnic to refer to these latter characteristics. Racial groups are groups which are thought to have a genetic or other deterministic base. Ethnic groups are thought of as those whose behaviour might change. Thus a group which has common cultural characteristics only (rather than common physical ones) may be termed a 'race' by those who oppose, oppress and exploit them, while a group which has clearly different physical characteristics may, those characteristics notwithstanding, be held by political democrats and liberals to be only ethnically different. We shall return to this theme in the next chapter.

Chapter 2

Race and Ethnicity in Sociological Theory

The Definition of Race and Ethnicity

The use of the terms 'race' and 'ethnicity' varies widely in popular and political discourse, so much so that it is difficult to promote a reasoned discussion about what would be the best use of the terms by a sociologist. In Nazi Germany, the Jews were declared to be a race; subsequently most writers suggested that they were 'only' an ethnic group. In the United States, earlier practice was to refer to ethnic differences between new European immigrants and longer settled White Americans, but to acknowledge that the difference between Blacks and Whites was racial. Later there was a tendency to regard all minorities, whether Black, Mexican or Native American and whether European, Latin American or Asian immigrant as 'ethnic'. In the United Kingdom, in a strange popular usage Black and Asian people were regarded as 'immigrants' whereas actual immigrants from Europe, Ireland and the White Commonwealth were not. As more positive attitudes towards the Blacks and Asians came to be adopted, they were referred to as 'ethnic minorities', along with other visible groups (like the Cypriots).

The various United Nations organizations, but particularly UNESCO, sought to resolve some of their problems after 1945 by commissioning first biologists and then social scientists to give an exact scientific meaning to the term race. Such a development was obviously important because of the malign political consequences which had resulted from the misuse of the concept.

While covering a great deal of other complex ground, the biologists concluded that the human species had a single origin and that the so-called races of mankind were statistically distinguishable groups only. Thus it was possible to classify groups of human beings in terms of the predominance of certain indices, such as the cephalic or nasal index, skin colour, hair type and so on, provided that one recognized considerable overlap between one group and another. It was not thought, however, that such physical differences were correlated with behavioural or psychological differences, hence the notion that 'race' could be used to *justify* unequal treatment was rejected. The concept of race as the biologist used it was seen to be irrelevant to the explanation of political differences amongst human beings, and it was suggested that the explanation why such differences were regarded as due to race was left to the sociologists (Hiernaux 1965).

Sociologists responded in three ways to this challenge. The first was to assimilate all so-called racial problems into the category of ethnic problems. The second was to recognize that racial differences did exist and often acted as markers for the differential apportionment of rights, but to limit the range of application of the term race and to deny that it had any justificatory significance. The third was to use the terms race relations situation to refer to situations marked by racism.

The first response reflected the same humane ethical and political stance involved in the change of usage noted in the opening paragraph. As such it was no doubt admirable. Unfortunately, as a means of classifying events and objects in the real world, it involved much wishful thinking. One might wish that all group differences involved only difference and not invidious distinction, discrimination and oppression, but, in fact, there was a distinction to be drawn between those benign cases where two ethnic groups were simply culturally different and those malign cases in which one group oppressed or exploited another. The attempt to assimilate racial to ethnic problems, therefore, often led to the interpretation of racial problems not as forms of conflict but as benign phenomena of difference.

The second alternative was to recognize that physical differences did exist and that they could act as markers for the assignment of rights to individuals. It could then be suggested that there were two types of situations involved, namely those in which 'racial groups' distinguished by phenotype were found and those in which the only differences were differences of culture. However, this approach did not distinguish the way in which phenotypical differences were treated in different situations. While most Black-White encounters in the modern world have been conflictual, some are more conflictual than others, and in few cases the phenotypical differences lead only to benign interaction. A sociology of race relations which classified the interaction between Black and White intellectuals in Paris together with the relations between Black and White in South Africa, for example, would be gravely misleading.

The third alternative seemed to group together those situations which were marked by severe conflict, exploitation, oppression and discrimination whether they were based on phenotypical markers or not, and to accept all of those situations which were marked by racist justifications as race relations situations. This was the alternative which I chose to adopt in my book *Race Relations in Sociological Theory* (1970) and repeated in other places (1973).

According to this view, three elements were involved in a 'race relations situation'. First, there was a situation of severe conflict, discrimination, exploitation or oppression, going beyond that which is normal in a free labour market. Secondly, this situation existed not simply between individuals but between whole categories of people (called quasi-groups in this text) so that the individual could not move at will from one category or quasi-group to the other. Thirdly, such a situation was justified by powerful groups in terms of some sort of deterministic theory (usually a biological or genetic one) which argued that the position of the different categories or quasi-groups could not be other than it was.

This was a deliberately perverse definition of the field of race relations designed to draw attention to a set of situations which were politically problematic. It was especially concerned to answer the problem posed by the UNESCO meetings (Montagu 1972): how to define the nature of the situations that gave rise to Anti-Semitism in Germany or to the doctrine and practice of White Supremacy in South Africa. The definition was, however, open to a number of objections. It gave no recognition to the differences between situations in which phenotype was the marker of role-obligations and those in which such markers were cultural. Secondly, it seemed to include many situations such as that which prevails in Northern Ireland between Roman Catholics and Protestants under the heading 'race-relations', which is a somewhat abnormal usage. And, thirdly, it does not seem to discriminate between situations of race and class conflict.

To the first of these criticisms, the reply might be that it does not matter whether all situations involving phenotypically different men and women are included in our study. They need only be included if they do lead to 'conflict, discrimination, exploitation or oppression'. This reply, however, has been thought too cavalier. Phenotypical differences, which are physical and visible, do provide a basis for making invidious distinctions that are much more difficult to challenge than cultural differences. The latter are more changeable and might be differently perceived at different times and in different situations. Thus, even if we insist that 'conflict, discrimination, exploitation and oppression' are of the essence of race relations situations, we might still distinguish within this category between those situations where the marker for role assignment is physical and those in which it is not.

The second objection could be rejected on the ground that it is far more important to notice the similarities between the Northern Ireland situation and situations of racial conflict, than it is to group the Northern Ireland situation with situations of benign ethnicity or to group together all racial situations whether conflictual or not. Nonetheless, it is useful perhaps to distinguish within situations of conflict between those marked by physical and those marked by cultural differences. If we may say for the sake of exposition that justificatory theories always involve lies, then the lie is different in the two cases. In the racial case it asserts falsely that physical differences which are real have behavioural or psychological correlates. In the ethnic case it asserts that behavioural and cultural differences are genetically determined.

The third problem raised is also serious. It could be argued, for example, that the condition of urban and rural workers during the industrial revolution in Britain fulfilled all the conditions suggested in my definitions. There was ultra-exploitation and oppression; there was, in Disraeli's words, a sense of 'two nations' not merely 'fed by a different food' but 'bred by a different breeding'.

I think I would have to concede that this was true at the outset of the industrial revolution and that the condition of the working classes in Britain then would fall within my definition of a race relations situation. But I would draw a distinction between situations which do not go beyond the level of severity of 'conflict, discrimination, exploitation and discrimination' in a free labour market and those which do. The point about the early stages of the industrial revolution is that it did not involve a free labour market. The worker could not go to seek a job with another employer or wait to choose. He was faced very often with a choice between accepting the employer's conditions or entering the essentially punitive workhouse.

My Marxist critics, however, might take exception that I distinguish between degrees of exploitation and perhaps deny that the free labour market really involves exploitation at all. Marx, it might be pointed out, specifically set out to suggest that the nation of a free labour market was a mystification of the reality and that there was actually a systematic extraction of surplus value from the workers.

In reply one might, of course, question the notion of surplus value and argue that, even if one does not accept the optimistic view of markets taken by exchange theorists, there is nonetheless a difference between market situations and exploitation and oppression of a direct sort. This other type of exploitation and oppression might occcur if there is no market situation at all or if it has broken down into the type of power confrontation referred to in Chapter 1. Also of importance, however, is the distinction between type of justification of exploitation used in capitalist societies with free labour markets and that used, for instance, in colonial societies. In the former case, the relation between employer and employee is represented and justified as a free market one. In the latter, the justification is of a different kind, often involving references to racial theory.

Possible Race and Ethnic Situations

Despite what has been said in defence of my definitions of a race relations situation in the above paragraphs however, it might be useful to make some further distinctions. In a later essay (Rex 1986) I have suggested that racial and ethnic situations might be conceived of as being located in four boxes somewhat as follows:

	Conflict situations	*Situations of relative harmony*
Group distinction on basis of phsyical (phenotypical) characteristics	Racial conflict A	Racial cooperation or interaction B
Group distinction on basis of cultural characteristics	Ethnic conflict C	Ethnic cooperation or interaction D

Figure 1. Types of racial and ethnic situation

In order to meet the criticism of those who suggest that some discrimination might be made between class conflict and conflict based on race and ethnicity, this table could in principle be extended to include a third row which refers to class thus:

Group distinction based on class or status	Class conflict E	Status system with consensual order F

Figure 2. Class and status in relation to racial and ethnic situations.

However, this suggests that racial and ethnic situations are devoid of class and status content. In fact, the table in Figure 1 already draws attention in its column heads to the element of conflict and order involved in racial and ethnic relations, and this is because the racial and ethnic groups may be related as classes, estates and status groups. Boxes E and F in Figure 2 may really only make sense in relation to classes and status groups which are devoid of ethnic content.

At all events, Figures 1 and 2 suggest that according to my own definition of the field of race and ethnic relations the situations with which we should deal belong in Boxes A, C and E. Many cultural anthropologists are more concerned with ethnic relations of kinds which fall into Boxes B, D and F.

What we have suggested so far is only the simplest mapping of our field. We have looked at racial, ethnic and class relations in terms of the dimension conflict/harmony. We should now note, however, that the notion implied in our new headings of 'group distinction' leaves open the question of who makes the distinction and whether both parties to a race or ethnic relations situation agree to the distinction made. If we take the boxes A and C, for example, it is possible that Group X may see Group Y as racially distinct, but that Group Y may regard itself as either not distinct or as ethnically distinct, or as distinct in class terms. Group Y might also disagree with Group X's diagnosis of the basis of its being distinguished. So we would have the following range of possibilities for Box A expressed diagrammatically (Figure 3).

To explicate this complex table somewhat, if there are two quasi-groups X and Y, X's members may see themselves as a race or an ethnic group, as a class or as not forming a category of any kind (i.e. being simply individuals). They may see the quasi-group Y as also forming a race, ethnic group or class or as not being a category at all. But there is no reason why they should see the other quasi-group as having the same character as their own. Thus X may see itself as ethnic and Y as a class group.

Y also makes its own valuations, and its categorization of itself may not be the same as its categorization of X. Even more important, Y's valuation of X may not be the same as X's valuation of itself.

A predominantly racial conflict		Group X's diagnosis of X and Y				Group Y's diagnosis of X and Y			
		Based on race	Based on ethnicity	Based on class	Not recognized as category	Based on race	Based on ethnicity	Based on class	Not recognized as category
	X	Based on race	Based on ethnicity	Based on class	Not recognized as category	Based on race	Based on ethnicity	Based on class	Not recognized as category
	Y	Based on race	Based on ethnicity	Based on class	Not recognized as category	Based on race	Based on ethnicity	Based on class	Not recognized as category

Figure 3. Complementarity or otherwise of inter-group categorization in predominantly racial conflicts

predominantly ethnic situations		Group X's diagnosis of X and Y				Group Y's diagnosis of X and Y			
		Based on race	Based on ethnicity	Based on class	Not recognized as category	Based on race	Based on ethnicity	Based on class	Not recognized as category
	X	Based on race	Based on ethnicity	Based on class	Not recognized as category	Based on race	Based on ethnicity	Based on class	Not recognized as category
	Y	Based on race	Based on ethnicity	Based on class	Not recognized as category	Based on race	Based on ethnicity	Based on class	Not recognized as category

Figure 4. Complementarity or otherwise of inter-group categorization in predominantly ethnic situations

In these circumstances we cannot call any situation completely racial unless both groups classify themselves and the others as races. We could, however, speak of a predominantly racial situa-tion when most of the self or other categorizations are racial.

A similar diagram can be drawn for predominantly ethnic conflicts (Figure 4).

One could also draw up a table for conflicts predominantly based on class (Box E). So far as Boxes B, D and F are concerned, the existence of relative harmony suggests that X's categorization of X and Y and Y's categorization of X and Y are normally in agreement, but a table could be drawn up for each of these in order to distinguish Race, Ethnicity, and Status systems and individual systems of status striving.

The column heading 'Based on Class' also serves to simplify a more complex reality. Quasi-groups may see each other not only as classes (in the Marxian or Weberian sense), but also as castes, estates, and status groups. Especially important here is the case in which the system is regarded as, and usually is, an estate system, which is a common case, as we shall see, in colonial societies. Insofar as such a system is based upon consensus, of course, it belongs in boxes B, D and F, but we should also note that estates do resist their assigned position so that there is a power struggle between estates.

Obviously any taxonomy of possible race relations situations is complex. The tables in Figure 4 would by themselves yield 256 theoretically possible cases and when the variation indicated in the last paragraph is taken into account there would be even more. But if this were not enough, the theorists of ethnicity have suggested even greater complexity.

Theories of Ethnicity

Much recent writing about ethnicity (Barth 1969, Wallman 1979) has emphasized a 'situational' view of ethnicity. This is developed in contrast to the 'primordial' view stated by Geertz:

> By a primordial attachment is meant one that stems from the 'givens' or more precisely, as culture is inevitably involved in such matters, the assumed 'givens' of social existence: immediate contiguity and live connection mainly, but beyond them the givenness that stems from being born into a particular religious community, speaking a particular language, or even a dialect of a language, and following particular social practices. These congruities of blood, speech, custom and so on, are seen to have an ineffable, and at

times, overpowering coerciveness in and of themselves. One is bound
to one's kinsman, one's neighbour, one's fellow believer, *ipso facto*,
as the result not merely of personal attraction, tactical necessity,
common interest or incurred moral obligation but at least in great
part by virtue of some unaccountable absolute import attributed to
the very tie itself.

(Geertz 1963, p.109)

Gordon suggests that this sense of ethnicity

because it cannot be shed by social mobility, as for instance social
class backgrounds can, since society insists on its inalienable ascrip-
tion from cradle to grave, becomes incorporated into the self.

(Gordon 1978, p. 73)

According to this view, ethnic ties cannot become too involved
with or dependent upon class or other political factors. They simply
cross-cut it. Moreover, if a quasi-group's assessment of its own
position (X's assessment of X or Y's assessment of Y) is based on
ethnicity, it will not be altered in the face of external pressures, and
so far as the assessment of other quasi-groups' position is concerned they are simply seen negatively as outgroups. Ethnicity thus
has its own dynamic independently of other elements in the
political process.

This is a challenging and important thesis which we should take
into account. It is, however, possible to recognize the existence of
purely ethnic bonding as an independent variable without saying
that it is the only source of political action. One can hold, for
example, that the Marxist notion of a process of a class-in-itself
becoming a class-for-itself will be asserted or facilitated by the existence of ethnic bonds which stand in the way of or sometimes
reinforce ties based on class interest. That is to say, we might agree
that ethnic quasi-groups exist for primordial reasons but also hold
that they can become part of a class system or cut across that class
system.

Against this theory, however, a theory of situational ethnicity
has been developed by some anthropologists. According to this,
not merely may ethnicity become a vehicle of class in macro-
situations; there will also be numerous much more specific contingencies in the face of which it may be invoked or not invoked.
It is misleading to speak of ethnic groups or even quasi-groups
according to this view. Ethnicity functions primarily as a resource.
It can be used to summon up a social organization for the attainment of ends when it is needed, but it can also simply be latent and
ignored.

Ethnicity according to this theory might not simply be a useful resource. It might be appealed to by other groups as a basis for denying rights. That is to say it might become a stigma or liability, which actually stands in the way of the members of a quasi-group attaining their ends.

There may be less disagreement between the theorists of situational ethnicity and the theory expounded here than first appears. It has been said above that ethnicity produces quasi-groups and that within these more specific associational activities may be envisaged. Surely this is not very different from saying that ethnicity is available as a resource for using in specific circumstances? The main difference between the two types of theory probably lies in the fact that the theorists of situational ethnicity play down the possibility of the overall mobilization of the resource of ethnicity in the interests of a class, and that they have failed to develop the other side of their theory, namely that which sees ethnicity as a stigma or a liability. I believe that these differences have to do with differences in the political perspectives of those involved. The theory of situational ethnicity has been developed by anthropologists who are not much concerned with political issues of class struggle and racism, while the approach adopted here sees the interplay between class, ethnicity and race, and the oppression and exploitation of racial and ethnic groups as its primary concern.

It would be unwise, however, to be dogmatic and sectarian about this. The kind of structural theory advanced here and the study of situational ethnicity are complementary rather than opposed. Structural theories deal with the macro-issues of the relations between classes, races and ethnic groups. The situational theory is concerned with the finer-grained work of looking at the here-and-now of specific situations. All we should say is that if we take such fine-grained work into account, the column heading 'class' in our table has to be broken down into a variety of sub-columns, so that instead of 256 possible cases we would have $256 \times X$. But such is the complexity of the social world, and sociologists must attune their theories to the world as it is.

Another development that has to be set against primordialism results from the use of the theory of rational choice in relation to racial and ethnic relations. According to this view, human beings are not to be thought of as acting in terms of 'givens' so that they act like automatons. What they will do is maximize their utility in accordance with their preference schedules. Moreover, each individual will have his own preference schedule. While organizations, groups and quasi-groups may exist and offer benefits, there is no reason why the individual should join them. He can simply take advantage of those benefits as a 'free-rider'.

The curious feature of such theories is that they do not seek to explain the existence of groups, quasi-groups or the ethnic resource. They simply take it for granted. If, however, we have a structural theory that explains the existence of such macro-structure, it is possible to see that rational-choice theory has a role within it as a means of explaining the behaviour of specific individuals or aggregates of individuals.

In the approach suggested in this book, the sociology of race and ethnic relations is concerned with the interaction of racial and ethnic quasi-groups, and it has been suggested that very often these relationships are imposed by the economic and political order. The actual quasi-groups which exist are based upon race and ethnicity (using that term to refer to the ties of kinship, common residence, common language, common religion and common customs, as suggested by Geertz), whether recognized by those who share them as a bond or imposed on them by others. We saw, moreover, that there was often a considerable disparity between the way a quasi-group saw itself and the way in which others saw it, and also between the way it saw other quasi-groups and the way in which they saw themselves.

We may refer to these disparities as forming the basis of a cognitive conflict and it is this type of conflict taken down to its finer-grained forms which preoccupies the theorists of ethnicity. This *is* of interest to the sociologist of race relations. Nonetheless, it is not merely a cognitive conflict about which quasi-group is what that is at stake in the theory of race and ethnic relations. Much more important are the real social conflicts which arise on the political and economic level between groups who see themselves regarded by others as racial and ethnic. This has been the concern of some of the major structural theories in sociology and to them we now turn. We shall deal first with the dispute about the nature of race relations in the United States between W. Lloyd Warner and Cox, then with the theory of the plural society and finally with the problems of Marxist theory when it is applied to race and ethnic relations.

Theories of Racial and Ethnic Group Conflict

W. Lloyd Warner (1936) offered a structural theory of the type with which we are most concerned to explain race relations in the United States. According to him, White America had a status order in which individuals moved, subject to some restrictions on mobility, from the lower, through the middle to the upper status groups.

(Warner called these groups 'classes'.) Blacks too had their status system, but even the Blacks who reached the highest status in Black society could not enter White society. Relations within the White and the Black community, Warner therefore suggested, where relations of class (we should say 'status') while the relation between Black and White was one of caste.

This could be expressed diagrammatically as follows:

	Upper Class	Relations
White	Middle class	of
		class
society		and
	Lower class	mobility

Caste
barrier

	Upper class	Relations
Black		of
	Middle class	class
society		and
		mobility
	Lower class	

Figure 5. Class and caste in America (Warner)

The size of the Black upper class was at first very small. When it increased, however, this did not mean that Blacks breached the caste barrier. This could be conceived of as tilting but not breaking down. Diagrammatically this is what happened:

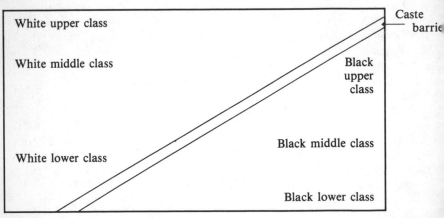

Figure 6. Black mobility and the caste barrier.

Oliver Cromwell Cox (1970), adopting what he regarded as a Marxist point of view, rejected the notion that it was a caste barrier between Black and White and suggested that the relations between Black and White were relations of exploited and exploiter, that is, of class. To justify this point of view, he gave a long and scholarly account of the Indian caste system, showing that it was based on occupational specialization and that its religious rationalization won for it a considerable measure of consent.

Interestingly enough, this dispute between Warner and Cox might be seen as a cognitive conflict between members of the White and Black quasi-groups. One sees the situation as one of caste, the other of class conflict. Obviously, too, there is the possibility which Cox, given his Marxist perspective, does not represent, of seeing the situation as one of race relations and race conflict. But the question of the nature of the relationship between Black and White is not merely a question of labelling. The important structural question is whether the relationship was in fact one of caste or whether it was one of class conflict. We should notice here that, according to Cox, what goes on within the White groups and within the Black group is status striving (or what Cox confusingly calls 'social class'), whereas the relations between the two races are those of economic class.

There are problems in Cox's view of this matter. In particular, one might well ask whether there are not also relations of economic class conflict within the White and the Black communities and, if there are, what the relationship is between the White working class and the Black. Here Warner's emphasis upon a caste-like barrier seems to be important, but the problem can be put into better focus if we give more attention to the relationship of various groups to the means of production. This is a complex question in the United States where, historically, there have been two modes of production and two societies, viz. that based on the slave plantation and that based on the exploitation of free immigrant labour. We shall return to this issue in the next chapter.

The notion that the relations between Black and White in the United States and elsewhere were those of caste or economic classes is further challenged by the theory of the plural society, whose principle advocates have been J. S. Furnivall and M. G. Smith.

Furnivall was a British colonial administrator who developed his theory in two books, *Netherlands India* (1939) and *Colonial Policy and Practice* (1968). In the former, he starts from the observation of the Dutch economist, J. H. Boeke, that in the case of colonial capitalism

> there is materialism, rationalism and individualism and a concen-
> tration on economic ends far more complete and absolute than in

homogeneous Western lands; total absorption in the Exchange and
Market; a capitalist structure with the business concern as the subject, far more typical of capitalism than one can imagine in the so-
called capitalist countries which have grown slowly out of the past
and are still bound to it by a hundred roots.

(Furnivall 1939, p. 452)

Furnivall agrees with Boeke that there is a sharp difference
between established European capitalism and capitalism of a
colonial sort. Boeke's words seem to suggest that the former is
characterized by market processes, but that these only come truly
into their own in the colonial case. This involves a slightly different
emphasis from mine in Chapter 1 where I distinguished market
processes from others and saw these as having the same
characteristics in all circumstances, but it has to be recognized that
there is a difference between the way in which there might be a direct
use of force superseding market relations and situations where this
is not possible. Under colonial conditions, market processes and
exploitation in the market clearly take a more brutal form. Weber
(1962) saw this when he wrote of 'booty capitalism' operating
under conditions of imperialism.

Furnivall, however, is only partly concerned with the absence of
'Social will' in the case of colonial capitalism. He is more concerned with its consequences, especially with the fact that the
various peoples are not bound together in a single unit by any kind
of normative bonds. As he puts it in his later book:

> In Burma, as in Java, probably the first thing that strikes the visitor
> is the medley of peoples—European, Chinese, Indian and native. It
> is in the strictest sense a medley for they mix but do not combine.
> Each group holds by its own religion , its own culture, its own ideas
> and ways. As individuals they meet, but only in the market place,
> in buying and selling. There is a plural society with different sections
> of the community living side by side but separately within the same
> political unit. Even in the economic sphere there is a division of
> labour on racial lines.

(1968, p. 304)

According to this account of the plural society, therefore, we
have a situation in which separate peoples or ethnic groups
organize their own separate communities held together by what
Geertz would claim are the primordial bonds of ethnicity. The
larger society, however, is one in which the pure laws of the market
hold, unrestrained by any sort of moral control. Moreover, this is
not just a matter of the relations between buyer and seller. It also
affects the division of labour, so that productive activity rests not
on some kind of moral order, as Durkheimian sociology suggests,

but upon crude market processes of the kind discussed in Chapter 1, which can very easily give way to processes of compulsion.

It should be noted that what we may call the 'villain' of Furnivall's piece is 'the market'. He does not draw attention to the fact that the economic relations of the colonial market place are often marked by the use of force, that is by the intersection of political and economic processes. Nor does he have a very clear conception of the social relations of production which, in colonial circumstances, as Weber had suggested with his concept of 'booty capitalism', are usually based upon force and the use of unfree labour. In these respects, the work of M. G. Smith would seem at first to be more helpful in that Smith lays primary emphasis upon the political order as the means of holding colonial society together.

Smith, who is primarily an anthropologist and, unusual within that discipline, a theorist, develops the idea of a plural society with a view, in the first place, to explaining Caribbean society. He begins by giving an anthropologist's account of the division between various plural segments. There is no attempt in Smith's work to give an account of the economy which brings these segments together. He does, however, give a detailed analysis of the meaning of cultural differentiation and offers his own theory of the institutional links between the segments. He does this with the aid of Malinowski's theory of institutions (Malinowski 1944).

According to Malinowski, a normal society has a basic set of institutional arrangements through which it meets its basic and derived needs. These include family systems, education, law, religion and economic organization. It is precisely the use of these institutional arrangements which unites men into a society. But in the case of the Caribbean, Smith argues there is no single society in this sense at all. It seems there are several different societies juxtaposed, each with its own complete institutional set.

In fact, however, the institutional set is not complete. None of the separate societies has its own political institution and the business of political regulation (very important on Malinowski's functionalist theory) falls to the dominant group. That is to say, the separate groups are bound together by the State. Smith further insists that the colonial state is not simply a sort of steering mechanism, through which shared values are realized. It is divorced from the values of the separate groups, but actually seems to impose the will of one group upon the others.

Emphasis in Smith's work is much more on political rather than economic factors as the source of interethnic interaction. There is strangely little reference to what Marxists call the 'mode of production'. Political processes are seen as both temporarily and

theoretically prior to the economic. It is because political domination by one group has occurred, usually through military conquest,
that the various ethnic segments occupy the position they do. The
key notion which comes to dominate Smith's theory, therefore, is
that of *de facto* differential incorporation. If Furnivall fails to emphasize the influence of political forces on the market, it would
appear that Smith goes to the other extreme. Political incorporation seems to exist *in vacuo*, divorced from any consideration of
economic purposes which might have brought the groups together
in the first place.

One writer in the plural society tradition who does bring together
the two elements of economic and political relations is Smith's
collaborator, Leo Kuper. Kuper's views have been conveniently
summarized by Banton as follows:

1. Societies composed of status groups or estates that are
   phenotypically distinguished, have different positions in the
   economic order, and are differentially incorporated into the
   political structure, are to be called plural societies and
   distinguished from class societies. In plural societies political relations influence relations to the means of production more than
   any influence in the reverse direction.

2. When conflicts develop in plural societies they follow the lines of
   racial cleavage more closely than those of class.

3. Racial categories in plural societies are historically conditional;
   they are shaped by intergroup competition and conflict.
                                                        (Banton 1983)

This is obviously a considered theoretical statement which does
justice to the role of the political, the economic and the racial
element in colonial social structure. It would also be applied to
groups distinguished by culture rather than by phenotype.

If Smith overemphasizes the political, it is to be expected that
Marxist theorists, starting from the importance of the 'mode of
production' as a factor structuring the relations between groups,
would overemphasize the economic (although it should be pointed
out that much recent Marxist thinking is very revisionist on this
point, Hall 1980).

For a long time, the characteristic Marxist view of colonial
society was that it was 'feudal' or 'pre-capitalist'. This view,
however, came to be criticized, as a new generation of Marxist
writers like A. G. Frank (1969) saw the whole colonial system as

integral to the development of capitalism. Underdevelopment in the colonial periphery, it was urged, was the other side of the coin to capitalist development at the centre.

This view, however, itself came in for criticism from Marxists. Frank's theory, as well as the world-systems theory of Wallerstein (1974), was seen as being concerned with understanding economic development rather than social structure and, hence, inclined to define capitalist social relations in terms of the market rather than in terms of the social relations of production. Brenner (1979) accuses Frank and Wallerstein of offering a Smithian (i.e. Adam Smith) rather than a Marxist theory of colonial society.

It has to be asked, however, what exactly is meant by the term 'mode of production' in colonial society. If the social relations of production which are integral to the mode of production are based upon conquest and the use of force, then no meaningful concept of the mode of production can be entertained which does not include political elements. Marxists could clearly be right in emphasizing that colonial societies were not simply systems of differentially incorporated estates and that some of the central conflicts in their societies were the consequences of men's differential relations to the means of production, but their concept of the mode of production had to be enlarged to include the political.

We are concerned here to establish the possible types of relations, particularly relations of conflict, which might be expected to exist between ethnic groups. Furnivall emphasized the market in the abstract; Smith emphasized 'differential political incorporation'; Marxists have emphasized the mode of production. In fact all three of these factors are involved. The 'mode of production' in a society based on conquest must include forms of differential incorporation and it would be unwise to assume that the labour market is the sole market involved in bringing different ethnic groups together. What is required is a theory of colonial society firmly based upon political economy.

How far is all this relevant to the theory of race and ethnic relations? Are we too readily abandoning the field to a modified form of economic determinism? The answer surely must be that race and ethnic relations and political and economic relations interact. We should note the following points:

(1) That the theory of race and ethnic relations must give an account not merely of why separate racial and ethnic groups form, but also of what brings them together. The latter type of theory may include some recognition of the fact that sheer cultural difference affects these relations; but it would be absurd to suggest that it can determine them. Clearly any realistic account of what

brings racial and ethnic groups together must refer to the structure of the polity and the economy.

(2) Even insofar as race and ethnicity are, of themselves, potentially important sources of in-group unity and intra-group division, their potential does require a structural content if it is to become activated. Racial and ethnic differences might very well be latent for long periods. When, however, groups or quasi-groups thus differentiated come into economic or political relations with each other, such latent relations become salient in a new way.

(3) If race and ethnicity have to be understood in relation to political and economic factors, however, the notion of classes and class conflict as well as that of estate systems and status group formations clearly requires recognition of racial and ethnic bonding. While the unity of interest groups and the division between opposed interest groups posited in any kind of conflict sociology (including the Marxist sociology of classes-in-themselves and classes-for-themselves) will normally be difficult to envisage as being achieved solely on the basis of the rational perception of common and opposed interests, such unity will be readily achieved when the groups concerned are in any case united by bonds of ethnicity and race.

Conclusion

We began this chapter by considering some of the difficulties in defining racial and ethnic situations. We saw that it was insufficient simply to distinguish between race and ethnicity by saying that one was based upon phenotypical, the other on cultural difference. Experience of race relations situations suggested that they were usually based upon severe conflict, discrimination, exploitation and oppression, whereas ethnic relations seemed to refer to benign conflict-free situations. Nonetheless, it seemed misleading to suggest that a situation of cultural and religious conflict, albeit with political overtones, like that in Northern Ireland, should be called a race relations situation. Hence it was suggested that it would be useful to make a four-fold distinction by cross-tabulating the degree of conflict and whether differences were physical or cultural.

It then became apparent that the classification of populations as races or ethnic groups or classes or the failure to generalize about them was partially at least a subjective matter and that, given the cognitions and belief-systems which groups had about each other, there could be many combinations of perception and misperception. It was also apparent that despite the existence of quasi-groups and despite the continuous availability of ethnicity as a resource, it only became salient in specific situations.

Sociological theories of race and ethnicity seemed to break down into two types. There were those which concentrated on cognition and immediate perceptions of the other in micro-situations and those which looked at interactions between quasi-groups structured at the macro-level. After looking at the conflict between Lloyd Warner and O. C. Cox, the theory of the plural society and arguments within Marxist theory, we concluded that the major structures in terms of which ethnic quasi-groups interacted involved market relations, including especially relations arising from relationship to the means of production, but also the type of political incorporation which prevailed.

Sociological theories in this field may also be distinguished by whether or not they concentrate on situations of conflict or situations of relative harmony. My intention here is to concentrate on the former because it is these which appear to be most problematic. It has been said with some truth that there is no such thing as good race relations, because if such existed we would not talk about them or be conscious of them. Given this emphasis, therefore, it seems to make sense to return to my original definition, while recognizing that both ethnic and race relations may occur within it. Thus we should say that our interest is in those situations in which (a) there is severe conflict, discrimination, exploitation or oppression (b) categories are clearly distinguished and it is relatively difficult for an individual to move from one category to another (c) the system is justified by some sort of deterministic theory.

These conditions appear to be fulfilled in colonial societies where most groups attain unequal rights within the society, while others remain outside, and in metropolitan societies or advanced industrial societies in which immigrants from colonial and dependent societies as well as refugees may not attain the legal, political and social rights which are normal in such societies. Chapter 3, therefore, deals with colonial societies and Chapter 4 with immigrant minorities in the metropolitan countries.

Chapter 3

Race, Ethnicity and the Structure of Colonial Society

This chapter and the next will be concerned with the circumstances in which quasi-groups distinguished by physical or cultural characteristics interact with each other in actual historical circumstances. It is not concerned with benign ethnicity or with those situations in which ethnicity is regarded as a resource. Rather it is concerned with situations in which ethnicity or race is, for the underdogs at least, a liability. It deals with situations of conflict, invidious discrimination, exploitation and oppression, and situations in which the deprivations of the exploited and oppressed are explained by those who dominate them as in some sense inevitable or natural. Thus, whether the oppressed and exploited group is defined racially or ethnically, what we call racism is present on the level of ideology.

The two preceding chapters have already shifted attention from aspects of quasi-group interaction which are due to race and ethnicity as such, though the existence of these aspects is admitted as one minor possibility, to the way in which this interaction is structured by systems of class, estate, status grouping, caste and individual status striving. But these are abstract possibilities only. In focusing on actual situations, most of the theorists of race have found it necessary to be still more specific and to indicate the actual types of historic circumstances in which malign racial and ethnic quasi-group interaction occurs.

Speaking of race relations Van den Berghe writes:

It seems that only when group differences in race overlap at least partially with dissimilarities in status and culture are these two sets of difference held to be causally related to one other.

(Van den Berghe 1967, p. 13)

That is to say that racist theory or ideology occurs in situations which, for other reasons, involve status differences. Van den Berghe then goes on:

These conditions are most clearly met when groups come into contact through migration of which the most common types are the following:

1. Military conquest, in which the victor (often in the numerical minority) establishes his political and economic domination over an indigenous group . . .

2. Gradual frontier expansion of one group which pushes back and exterminates the local population . . .

3. Involuntary migration in which a slave or indentured alien group is introduced into a country to constitute a servile caste . . .

4. Voluntary migration when alien groups move into the host country to seek political protection or economic opportunity.

(ibid. p. 14)

Richard Schermerhorn in his systematic *Comparative Ethnic Relations* (1970) finds it necessary to refer to what he calls 'repeatable sequences of interaction between subordinate ethnics and dominant groups'. These are (1) the emergence of pariahs, (2) the emergence of indigenous isolates (3) annexation (4) migration (5) colonization. Included under migration are (a) slave transfers (b) movements of forced labour (c) contract labour transfers (d) reception of displaced persons (e) admission of voluntary immigrants.

In my own earlier writing, too, I listed a number of historical contents of race relations situations. These included (1) frontier situations (2) slave plantations and post-plantation societies (3) situations of severe class conflict (4) estate and caste systems (5) status systems (6) situations of cultural pluralism. All of these I saw as occurring in colonial situations. I also went on, however, to refer to situations in metropolitan societies, including complex systems of urban stratification, pariah situations and scapegoat situations (Rex 1973).

It now appears to me to be possible to set out these historic situations more systematically in terms of a theory. I would suggest that

the variety of situations we encounter are the product of the interaction and contrast between the following: metropolitan and
colonial society, pre-colonial social forms and forms of colonial
exploitation, the economy and the polity, the original colonial
society and processes of modernization and change. This can be
made clear with the aid of the following table which distinguishes
in the case of colonial society between constitutive and processual
variables (Figure 7).

We should now look at each of these headings in turn.

Metropolitan societies will be considered in the next chapter.
They are distinguished from colonial societies by the fact that they
are based upon free labour markets and subsequent class struggle.
As we have seen, it is characteristic of colonial societies that they
involve in some measure the use of force, so that the relations
between employer and employed are not simply market relations.

Colonial societies will vary amongst themselves, in the first place,
according to the pre-existing pre-colonial social forms.

Pre-Colonial Social Forms

Political ideology, including racist ideology, has affected the
understanding of European scholars of the role of pre-colonial
social forms in the colonial and post-colonial period. At first it was
fashionable to emphasize this role in order to denigrate colonial
people. They were represented as heathens, irredeemably different
from Europeans and out of the mainstream of civilization. Against
such views radicals argued that coloured peoples had the same
needs as Europeans, that their societies were essentially the same
and that the emphasis on archaic differences was simply a means
of mystifying the process of exploitation. But this emphasis on the
rationality of colonial society in turn led to a racist type of theory.
Pre-colonial societies were regarded as having no value in themselves. Their way forward was seen as necessarily similar to that of
Western Europe, and unless European type institutions were
developed within them it was thought that they could only be
destined to stagnation. This was a view shared by Marx who saw
Oriental Despotism and the Asiatic Mode of Production as
obstacles to development, and Weber who emphasized the differences between Oriental Mysticism and the Rational Asceticism of
the West. Not surprisingly, Third World scholars in recent times
have raised the question of whether non-Western social forms
might not be compatible with progress, albeit in different directions
from that suggested by the formal rationality of the West.

In fact there are two very good reasons for giving attention to the variety of pre-colonial social forms. One is that the kind of colonial society which is possible will depend upon the kinds of social structure and institutions available for manipulation by the colonists. The other is that in the post-colonial period the institutional development of these societies might very well be affected by a revival of earlier forms suppressed under colonization.

The range of social, economic and political types amongst the societies colonized by Europeans is enormous. At one extreme there are small bands of nomadic hunters, such as were encountered by the Hudson's Bay Company in Canada. At the other are the great imperial systems of the East, such as the Moghul Empire in India. Many of the simpler and even some of the more complex societies were simply destroyed, marginalized or rendered dependent on colonialism. In the great Empires, on the other hand, colonizers often moved into exploitative roles already existing in complex and differentiated social systems and used the very institutions of those societies to exploit them.

The ultimate in colonial destruction was achieved in Tasmania and in the Caribbean where local people were either exterminated or died out after European settlement. In other cases the more simply organized peoples were cheated out of their land, denied all that was essential to the continuation of their way of life and eventually confined to reservations where their cultures survived only in attenuated form. Another alternative was to move large numbers of the tribal peoples into specially created settlements, like those created by the Jesuits in Paraguay or some of the missions in East Africa, where they could be trained and conditioned to a way of life appropriate to colonialism and quite distinct from their own.

An intermediate social type was achieved by the Bronze Age civilizations of Central America. Here again, however, the colonialists set about the systematic destruction of the societies and the cultures which they encountered. The precious products of these civilizations were merely taken as plunder and the ancient systems of labour exploitation replaced by institutions like the *encomienda*, which assigned 'Indians' as workers to Spanish settlers. The language and religion of these high cultures were largely destroyed and the inhabitants of the Empires either Hispanicized or reduced to a status not unlike that of other North American 'Indians'.

The peoples of West, East, Central and South Africa were usually organized in tribal confederations and nations, and in many places produced centralized states and empires. They never lost their languages under colonialism and there was no possibility of the total disappearance of the peoples or their cultures. A pattern

Metropolitan capitalist societies	Constitutive variables	Colonial societies		
		Pre-colonial social forms	Modes of exploitation	The order of colonial estates
Capitalist enterprises employing free labour leading to class struggle, possible social revolution and the welfare state. Subsequent employment of Immigrant labour as 'Underclass'.		These range from bands of nomadic hunters through tribal states to complex empires (e.g. Moghul Empire in India)	Unequal exchange Tax farming and military exploitation Exploitation of primary producers through marketing Manorial systems Latifundia and estate systems Plantations and mines using unfree labour (slaves and indentured workers)	Possible estates include (1) Planters (2) Rentiers (3) Slaves and indentured workers (4) Peasants (5) Share croppers and squatters (6) Unincorporated natives (7) Freemen, including freed slaves, coloureds and poor whites (8) Secondary traders (9) Free white workers; capitalists and farmers (10) Missionaries (11) Administrators

	Type of process	Variety of forms	Effect on class and estate systems
Processual variables	Economic liberalization	Slave emancipation Land reform Free trade	Move from fixed status to mobility and contract Emergence of new lower strata
	Political independence	Settler bourgeois rule Native bourgeois rule One party state	Emergence of political élites and Independent capitalists Also neo-capitalism
	Incorporation into world economic system	Subordination of local and Imperial capitalism to multi-national corporations	Neo-colonial élites Comprador Bourgeoisie Emergence of free proletariot
	Processes or revolution	Late struggle for political independence, nationalism and socialism	Military coups Alliances with superpowers Worker and peasant revolt
	The racial ordering of society	Structuring of social relations though racial ideology rather than law.	Racial; class and status systems

Figure 7. Structural factors affecting the racial and ethnic order in metropolitan and colonial societies

of indirect rule emerged that was in effect a form of feudalism in which native kings and princes acknowledged the authority of a colonial power and offered tribute, but were allowed to preserve their own institutions under the protection of the colonialist. The institutions of tribal war and slavery, moreover, were used by the merchants of West Africa to provide labour for the plantation economy of the Americas.

The African slaves themselves represent a polar case in the history of the survival or non-survival of pre-colonial cultures. The destruction of family life and the harsh quasi-military disciplines of the plantation made any process of cultural transmission very difficult, if not impossible. It is of interest to note that something did survive; even more important than these survivals, however, was a growing resistance to cultural dependency that eventually produced an ideological counter to racism and colonial domination in the form of the ideologies of Black Consciousness, Black Identity and Negritude.

Finally, there were the great empires and civilizations to the East. These had their own great religions, their own orders of caste, estate and class, their own patterns of production, exploitation and government, and their own networks of trade. Such civilizations could not be destroyed by colonization. Instead the colonialists moved into controlling positions in the society's institutions, subverting the civilization from the inside. The East India Companies, for example, took over from the Zamindar class and the princes the functions of the tax-gatherer and merchant-trader. Eventually the process of internal subversion transformed the social and political systems of South Asia, but never completely. Post-colonial India inherited a social system shaped by many traditional institutions, and the units of the new system were often cultures and societies shaped by traditional notions of caste and traditional religions.

Modes of Exploitation

Weber in his General Economic History (1962) and writings on the ancient world (1976) makes a distinction between Occidental capitalism, 'peacefully oriented to market opportunity', and the adventurer and booty capitalism of empire. The principal sorts of enterprise associated with this adventurer and booty capitalism were the financing of voyages and wars, tax-farming and the capitalistic development of the manor, which took the form either of estate-farming or of a plantation system.

Set up in the sixteenth century, a time that Wallerstein (1974) identifies with the emergence of the modern world system, the chartered companies were essentially a revival of an institution of the ancient world. The European merchants who formed companies did not merely engage in trade, but rather obtained the right to gather taxes, and with this, the right to govern and obtain monopoly privileges in trade. Such companies were formed in the sixteenth century primarily to deal with the exploitation of the East, although another type also developed in North America, and the institution was revived with the development of the Second British Empire in Africa.

The original *raison d'etre* of the companies in the sixteenth century was long-distance trade, but this was not the most important form of exploitation. It can indeed be argued that such trade was not necessarily unequal from the point of view of the colonial people. Far more important was the assumption of the tax-gathering function. The right to gather taxes was conceded by the Moghul emperors, which in turn brought the right to govern and use military force as well as allowing companies collectively and the company servants individually to engage in internal trade. This was the major form of exploitation in India until the Mutiny. The Crown then took over the Company's powers and the economies of Britain and India became interlocked. At this point India came to be both a market and a field for investment for British capitalism.

A very different pattern emerged in Latin America following the overthrow of the Central American empires. The Spanish and Portuguese sought more than anything else the establishment of manors and their own installation as a feudal nobility. The native people were either assigned to the settlers under the institution of the *encomienda* or they were engulfed and became squatters or tenants in the *latifundia*. Even there the extensive estate was not the rule as in Brazil where, however, the settlement type known as the Big House (Freyre 1963) was essentially concerned with production for the master's table rather than the market.

Such institutions were, of course, feudal in character, but in most cases they came under pressure from capitalism. In North America this led to a form of slavery which Elkins (1959) saw as involving 'the logic of unrestrained capitalism', but whenever there was an opportunity in the market, the institution of the hacienda or plantation or *latifundia*, which was in principle a manor, could be developed in a capitalist direction through the exploitation of slaves or by rent-farming.

There is some inconsistency in Weber's treatment of slavery. On the one hand he sees it as incompatible with capitalism, but on the other he sees the slave plantation as one of the main forms of the capitalistic development of the manor. Though slavery is an inflexible form unsuitable for adjusting costs during times of recession, nevertheless it would seem that in suitable market conditions it is a highly rational enterprise in which costs can be made more calculable because of the degree of labour discipline. It is hardly surprising then that econometricians have been able to show that North American slavery was a highly efficient economic system.

Plantation agriculture, like mining, is highly labour-intensive. For both, slavery is a highly efficient element in production. Even when slaves cease to be available, moreover, the institution of indentured or contract labour provides a new source of unfree labour. Hugh Tinker (1974) has rightly called such indentures a new system of slavery. Indentures, however, have the advantage over slavery of being more efficient because they are more flexible. When the contract period is reduced, as it is in South Africa from five years to nine months, employers can enjoy all the advantages of tight labour discipline without having responsibility for workers in times of recession and without any responsibility for the reproduction of the labour force.

The most widespread form of exploitation in the world, and not only in colonial societies, is the exploitation of peasants. Strictly speaking, a subsistence farmer who employs no one and fully feeds himself and his family is a peasant and, in fact, stands outside all feudal and capitalist systems. But as soon as subsistence agriculture has to coexist with other systems, peasants come under pressure. The farmer seeks to provide basic family necessities which cannot be provided from his own production, and this must involve exchanging part of his product. At the same time, population expansion and settlement by colonizers means that less and less land is available. Eventually any kind of economic independence is impossible and he has in part at least to abandon subsistence agriculture as a way of life and to become a share cropper, or peon, or a wage labourer. Peasant production is rarely independent of other systems. Sometimes its incorporation is more or less total, as in the South African migrant labour system, but other forms of colonial capitalism serve to incorporate the peasant into a wider economic world.

The reason for considering all these types of production, what Weber calls the institution of booty capitalism, is that it is useful to accept the general Marxist proposition that men's relation to the means of production determines their class position. If we are concerned with the likely development of class struggle in colonial society, however, we need to recognize that there is no possibility of a simple unidimensional division of the population into three classes of landowners, capitalists and proletarians. Each colonial society will have its own basic mode of exploitation, and it may be that many possible relationships to the means of production will mean a many-faceted class struggle. Within this complex pattern of class struggle, moreover, racial and ethnic quasi-groups confront each other, for race and ethnicity are what Banton calls the role signs (1967) which lead to the assignment of positions in the overall system of exploitation.

One point that should be noticed here is that the Marxist concept of the 'mode of production', if it is to be retained at all, has to be considerably extended if it is to account for these complex structures. The positions we are discussing are not simply positions defined in relation to the means of production, narrowly conceived. They also depend upon the access of individuals to the use of power. We are not simply discussing market relations or even only labour market relations. It would be best, therefore, if we were to speak of the relations of different categories of individuals to the political and economic apparatus.

So far, the kind of power struggle we have been discussing is a struggle about *de facto* power and this it often is. We should notice, however, that the position of the plantation slave, and often the position of a tenant farmer, is legally differentiated from that of the slave master or landowner. The struggle between classes also becomes in part a struggle between estates.

The Order of Colonial Estates

Although we have found that the class struggle in colonial societies is also a struggle not merely about *de facto* but *de jure* power, we have so far concentrated our attention on the major mode of exploitation in a society. But the quasi-groups who provide the personnel for this mode of exploitation do not constitute the whole of colonial society. Other positions and other quasi-groups are involved, partly because more goes on in these socieites than can be understood under the heading of 'the mode of exploitation' and partly because the functioning of that very mode of exploitation requires the existence of other roles and other categories of individuals to perform them. We shall see that even in the simplest imaginable case this leads to the establishment of a wider estate order.

It is worth pointing out here that we must necessarily simplify our model before we can look at more complex types. We shall therefore look at the model of a colonial society based upon a fairly simple case of plantations and *latifundia*. Later we will consider the implications for race relations theory where either what we shall call native society or settler society come to exercise more influence than the system dominated by planters and landlords.

We will first assume that the planters and landlords have special rights granted to them, particularly the rights of landownership, which distinguish them from other free men. Their monopolistic position gives them an interest distinct from that of other entre-preneurs. They may and usually do aspire to the feudal status of lords of manors, but they may seek to turn their monopoly to advantage when market opportunities occur.

The pure peasant is one who lives outside the *latifundia* but is dependent upon it. He is often difficult to distinguish, however, from the serf, squatter or share cropper who lives on the *latifundia*. All these groups are recognized by the law as having a dependent status.

Unlike the true peasants and the unfree tenants of the *latifundia* are the native people living within a colonial territory who have not been incorporated into the colonial order. They retain their economic independence, their own social institutions and their culture. The penetration of their society which might occur later will often require some sort of indirect rule and the use of their own social institutions.

The most crucial distinct status in colonial society is that of the slave. At the extreme, he is not thought of as a man at all, but as property or as a tool. He has no existence as an individual before the courts. We should note, however, the gradations of slavery amongst those who are in no sense free men, ranging from the status of the pure chattel slave working on the field to that of the house slave who might be accorded considerable *de facto* rights by his master.

No slave system exists for long, however, that does not produce free men on the margins. These fall into three groups: the offspring of sexual unions between planters and slave women; slaves who for some reason have been given their freedom; and poor whites whose racial affinity with the planter and landowning classes prevent them being classified as slaves, but whose lack of property and economic dependence makes them difficult to distinguish in other than racial terms.

The rules developed for dealing with these groups are of momen-tous importance in the later development of colonial society. So long as a proper estate system exists, they are all legally free persons, although without the rights of property owners. But distinctions in custom are made between them which come to have structural importance where the estate system is abolished. These distinctions may take a number of alternative forms. The masters who are the fathers may acknowledge their offspring and pass on rights to them. (This is rare and is only partially realized with some privileged coloureds being accorded rights, but when it does occur the dominant group in the society becomes mestizzised and coloured.) Secondly, the opposite rule may be adopted and the coloured offspring assigned to the status of slaves, thus clearly distinguishing them both from manumitted slaves and poor whites. A third alternative is to recognize groups of intermediate colour, either as was done in South Africa by recognizing a single coloured group or as in Mexico at one point in its history, where a whole range of so-called castes were distinguished by colour.

A different kind of departure from the basic system of plantation slavery occurs (usually after slave emancipation) with the introduction of indentured or contract workers. Often the terms of their indentures are such that even when their contract period is at an end they are forced to accept a *de facto* dependent status. Nonetheless, both during and after their period of indenture they form a distinct estate, distinguished both from slaves and other free men.

The economic servicing of the plantation through the provision of trade goods is rarely completely provided either by the planters themselves or by people who share their race and ethnicity. Such trade is often thought to be beneath their dignity and sometimes to involve economic behaviour which is morally unacceptable. Just as the Jews in medieval Europe performed this function for Christians, so it is performed in European-dominated colonial societies not merely by Jews, but by Indians, Syrians, Lebanese and by many of the minor European nations. The rights of this group may be only ambiguously defined at first, but usually they come to have a distinct legal status as well as a quite distinct community life. Such legal and social distinctions are reinforced by ethnic difference.

Colonies provide opportunities, however, not merely for such secondary pariah traders, but for other settlers from the metropolis. These will include those who become free farmers, workers and entrepreneurs. Potentially there are considerable class differences and class conflicts within this category, but so long as their numbers are small they simply form a separate estate of settlers, distinguished in custom if not in law both from the planters and owners of *latifundia* and from the poor whites.

Finally, two other categories of individuals perform a distinct social function in colonial society and like the secondary traders and the settlers they have a very distinct social life. Missionaries assume the task of converting the natives and seek to provide moral rationalization and criticism of colonial practice, and administrators represent the interest of the metropolitan government as distinct from that of the plantocracy and the settlers. It would be foolish to suggest that such missionaries and administrators do not at times connive with the powerful planter and settler groups to facilitate the exploitation of slaves, peasants and natives. But it would be wrong to suggest that this is all they do, and culturally, socially and legally they may be thought of as independent estates.

The order of estates may sometimes operate as a system of functioning parts, just as could the system of estates in medieval Europe. In particular it is clear that the rationalizing role of the missionaries and adminstrators serves to bring the estates together in a working relationship. Nonetheless such rationalization is most effective on the level of ideology rather than of actual practice, and the different estates may also be thought of as having their own interests which they pursue in conflict with one another. In these confrontations problems of ethnic and race relations arise between the quasi-groups which have been assigned particular legal as well as economic positions.

The model outlined in the last paragraph, however, is a model only of a past case of colonial society. In that model it is suggested that the various racial and ethnic categories and quasi-groups have no other role than that which follows from the colonial encounter. It fits best the constructed colonial societies of the Americas where the native people have either been exterminated and consigned to reservations, where a new servile population has been imported and cut off from its cultural heritage and where the numbers of free settlers from the metropolis are too small for a predominantly settler colony to be created.

Another possibility, of course, is that many of the native people remain outside the economic and cultural influence of the colonial society, even though recognizing the suzerainty of the colonial government and that even amongst those who do, native social institutions are preserved. In such a society ethnic and racial conflict will be limited to that which already exists in the more complex native society or which arises where particular groups have been assigned a role by the colonialist. If there is no large settler population, the most obvious type of racial contact involving racism will be that between the élite administrators and the people as a whole.

India provides an example of a colonial society of this kind. Precolonial society (or one should say the society which existed before the *British* intrusion) is complex and contains many quasi-groups divided by language, religion and culture. Cross-cutting this again, the society as a whole is organized into castes. Further conflicts have arisen because of the adoption of policies of alliance with or opposition to the colonialists. The administrators, first of the company and then of the metropolitan government, rule this society from a social position that is segregated from contact with the main society by a wide range of social taboos and through segregated industrial areas. The Anglo-Indian half-caste population which emerges from illicit sexual unions is assigned a position between that of the administrators and the natives. Finally, it should be added, such a society allows for considerable economic differentiation between people in native society, and native rulers may acquire great wealth.

Another possible type of colonial society is that in which free metropolitan settlers arrive in such numbers as to overwhelm the simple institutions of the plantation type of colony. This occurred more obviously in North America where a society based upon European immigrant labour arose alongside of the older plantation colonies. The European immigrant communities formed ethnic blocs during their period of settlement and were to some extent involved in ethnic conflict. These conflicts were mild, however, compared with the conflict between White and Black both in the old plantation colonies and when Blacks migrated to the settler societies of the North.

Another variant of the settler society occcurred in South Africa. Here, settler numbers were relatively smaller (about 20 per cent of the total population compared with 90 per cent in the United States) and it is harder to distinguish between the *latifundists* and free settlers. The original split in the society was between company employers and so-called 'free burghers', but these free burghers were themselves large-scale estate farmers who incorporated the natives on their lands as squatters. Moreover, the dominant industry of the society, diamond and gold-mining, operated along booty capitalist lines with the mine owners in a position equivalent to that of plantation owners. When new settlers arrived to work in newer, more modern industries, they often found that the earlier patterns of behaviour towards the natives were so strong that they simply adopted them. It took more than fifty years after the establishment of the gold mines before the practices of the new settlers began to conflict with those of the European farmers and the mine owners. Such a society was very productive of racial conflict and racism. Slavery played only a small part in South African history. In the main the natives were kept 'in their place' by the practice of racial domination and segregation. Intermediate places were assigned to Coloureds and to immigrant Indians (both indentured workers and secondary traders).

Economic Liberalization

The institutions of colonialism we have been discussing pre-dated the new world of *laissez-faire* which followed the industrial revolution in Britain and elsewhere. Slave plantations, *latifundia*, tax-farming and colonial mining enterprise lived in a world of monopoly. The new order being born in the metropolis and that which was sometimes espoused by free settlers in the colonies, however, was based upon the notion of free markets and competition. It had no place for slavery, for large rural estates or for economic privileges based upon the use of political force.

This had serious implications for the colonies. The movement for slave emancipation got under way and eventually led to the end of the institution. Land reform was demanded. Governments intervened to take over from the chartered companies. In principle, all of these developments should have individualized the social order and destroyed both ethnic and racial groups and the kinds of conflict which went with them.

In part, indeed, it did. But race and ethnicity as principles of social organization did not yield easily. In fact, since the various markets which were established were far from free, they rapidly gave way to collective bargaining and political conflict, and race and ethnicity were often the binding forces in the quasi-groups which pursued this conflict. Moreover, those who were set free as workers or farmers quickly found that they were in no position to compete. Ex-slaves migrating to the city to find work found that jobs were being filled by European workers who were more skilled and who in any case were preferred by employers of their own race. Dependent peasants and tenants given land found that they could not compete with settler farmers who had capital, skills and marketing opportunities. All too often, therefore, those who were newly liberated sank to the bottom of society and new racist theories were developed which explained their failure in terms of race and ethnicity.

Political Independence

M. G. Smith's theory of the plural society, it will be remembered, argued that the various ethnic and racial segments were held together by the political institution and this meant in effect political domination by one of the segments. Under colonialism this meant the monopolization of political power by the metropolitan power. When, however, colonialism was ended there was a danger of the society falling apart unless one of the segments could assert its own political domination.

This problem did not arise so sharply in the first moves towards political independence in the American colonies. Here settler rule and to some extent, within that, bourgeois rule, replaced metropolitan government. From the point of view of racial and ethnic relations, therefore, this meant little change. If anything it meant that settlers would have a greater measure of independence in competition with and in the exploitation of native and slave-descended populations.

In the case of India and to some extent in the case of the other Asian colonies, power was yielded to a native ruling class or bourgeoisie. This probably meant greater unity insofar as the new political élite was racially similar to the population which it ruled. In India religious and other ethnic divisions, however, remained, and it actually proved impossible to hold the state together. A Hindu élite and a Muslim élite could not rule together; nor was it possible for one to usurp power and rule over the other. The outcome was the creation of the states of India and Pakistan, and within each the élite confronted further ethnic, linguistic and religious divisions.

In the third type of case, independence was granted not so much because it was demanded and seized by a powerful class or ethnic group, but because the former metropolitan power was no longer able to command the financial and military resources necessary to assert its authority. Power was then handed over to the nationalist political organization of the native majority.

Usually the new governing group lacked the financial means to rule itself and entered into alliance with, and represented the interests of, overseas capital, so that metropolitan rule continued in a concealed form. But in any case such governments often faced problems in dealing with their own ethnic and racial minorities. This was particularly true for the Asian minorities in Africa. They had come in under the protection of the colonial power and now found themselves governed by the African majority. Where such a minority was powerful enough, it entered into an arrangement whereby its economic role was respected in return for its recognition of the right of the majority to govern. Such arrangements were always precarious and might easily break down in the form of violent racial attacks as in Uganda or in periodic racial disturbances as had happened outstide Africa, in Guyana and Malaysia. Generally it was to be expected that independence in territories of this type would lead to an increase in racial conflict.

Incorporation into the World System

The argument which has been advanced here takes for granted the fact of empire. It is always assumed that the governing power in colonial territories is that of a metropolitan *government*, ultimately more effective and powerful than the influence of non-nationally based capitalist entrepreneurship. It is under such governing arrangements that the various ethnic and racial quasi-groups encounter each other and under which ethnic and racial conflict occurs. This is an argument at odds with the view of Immanuel Wallerstein (1974) who goes out of his way to insist that empire as such is not important and that the overarching economic structure to which we are all subject is that of the 'Modern World System', in which domination has passed from governments to the multi-national corporations.

There is obviously some value in Wallerstein's perspective as an ideal type. The world is not structured simply by governments and it is useful, therefore, to work out what it would be like to live in a world structured instead by non-national capitalist corporations. But it is not historically true that empires were never important. They provided the structure that originally determined the experience of and shaped the attitudes of the various classes, races and ethnic groups.

What is true, however, is that, as imperial power declined, the destiny of the former colonial territories came to depend less upon the European governments and more upon the policies of corporations. In some cases this involved a former colony changing its metropolitan power as, for example, the Latin American colonies, having shaken off Portuguese and Spanish power, came more and more to be dominated by the United States. Sometimes it meant subordination to a group of states like the European Economic Community which represented the former imperial interests of a group of powers. But sometimes there was no clear metropolitan centre of authority at all and newly independent states had to deal directly with the corporations themselves. What effect, we must now ask, did this change have on ethnic and race relations in the emerging 'world systems'?

Multi-national corporations are seen by many people and political parties to be responsible for a multitude of the world's ills.

This is not surprising, because an interest in pure profit means they are likely to be even more insensitive than governments to the interests of other groups. But this by no means implies that they will be more likely to employ racial or ethnic domination as a tool. In fact, they may be insensitive to demands for the continuation of such domination. This is the most likely outcome if we imagine the corporations putting profit before all else. On the other hand, these corporations, like earlier forms of capitalism, are likely to take the line of least resistance. If a system of racial domination is most effective in promoting profit they will support it, but, if not, then they will be ruthless in supporting its overthrow.

Forms of Colonial Revolution

The order imposed by modern capitalist enterprise and post-colonial government on multi-racial and multi-ethnic societies should not be thought of as static. The new order and the remnants of the old colonial order implicit in it will be resisted by popular revolutionary forces. But even in these revolutionary forces one can see conflicts between different tendencies equivalent to the differences between the old colonial order and *laissez-faire* capitalism.

As the colonial economy becomes incorporated into the world capitalist order, so the forces of revolution become drawn to the world revolution against capitalism. Political parties arise which explain the exploitation of the colonial worker as capitalist-led class exploitation and invite him to throw in his lot with the international working class. Such Marxist parties also denounce the purely nationalist leaders of the revolt against colonialism as a comprador bourgeoisie. For them the colonial worker can only be liberated when he is liberated from capitalism itself.

Colonial Nationalism, however, has developed its own theories to oppose these notions, particularly in territories where liberation from colonialism was delayed. Thus Frantz Fanon, a native of Martinique and theorist of the Algerian revolution, came to give a coherent account from a nationalist point of view of the colonial revolution which was strongly opposed to Marxism (1965).

Fanon's teacher Aimee Cesaire had stated in his letter of resignation from the French Communist Party that the liberation of the French proletariat was not the primary aim of the people of Martinique, and Fanon, in the light of his own experience of collaboration with the French Communist Party, came to see that Algerian nationalists as such had far more in common with each other than did Algerian workers with the workers of France. He therefore urged Algerians regardless of class to back the national revolution until the French were expelled. Only after that struggle had been won did he envisage the settling of accounts by the Algerian workers with their own probably neo-colonial bourgeoisie.

It is not necessarily of concern to us here whether Marxism or Fanonism is right. What matters is that whereas Marxism preaches a universalist and non-racist creed, Fanonism (in a variety of forms and not only in the doctrines of Fanon himself) sets the nationalist ethnic and racial unity of the exploited colonial peoples against their metropolitan masters who are clearly distinguished by their skin colour. Fanon specifically urges Black men to abandon 'white masks' (1952) and in his acceptance of the inevitability of violence channels all the hostilities of Black colonial people against their White masters. Though he would undoubtedly see his own doctrine as anti-racist, it is clear that this revolutionary doctrine involves a categorization of the rulers in racial terms and the alliance of colonial forces on an ethnic and racial basis.

This kind of mobilization of the colonial revolution also takes other forms. Deprived of their ancestral culture and forced to see themselves from the point of view of White culture as the inferiors of White men, many Black leaders in recent times have preached the doctrines of Black Consciousness, Black Pride and the simple notion that Black is Beautiful. They have also, following the teachings of Garvey, revived the idea of a return to Africa. Here Blackness ceases to be a 'liability' imposed on Black people by White categorization. It becomes the chosen form of identification for Black people themselves. Of course, like Marxism's myth that working men will come to identify primarily as workers and part of the international working class, so also this myth is only partially realized in the consciousness of those to whom it is supposed to refer. It is nonetheless important to recognize that it is a major reference point in the policies of the colonial revolution and past colonial society.

The Racial Ordering of Society

The paradox of the modernization and individualization of colonial and post-colonial society lies in the fact that though it is based upon universalistic notions, racial categorization may become more rather than less important within it. Where there is the legal differential incorporation of groups, which is to be found in an estate system, there is no need for racial categorization as such. If, however, there is a structural need for differentiation after its legal basis has beeen destroyed, then the differentiation will be justified on ideological grounds. Racial ideologists provide a ready source of such justifications. The most obvious case is in the American Deep South where emancipation after the Civil War was at odds with the beliefs of White Southern Society. Law was therefore replaced by the set of discriminatory and segregatory practices known as Jim Crow. Through these practices, the society was structured not along lines of legal differentiation, but on grounds of race and colour.

We shall be concerned in later chapters with the question of whether such racial categorization and such racial practices are inevitable or whether they can be overcome either by the universalistic principles of modern democratic nation-state or by confrontation with resistance from the dominated part of society. Here we need only record that in societies which start from a colonial base there are many possible sources of racial and ethnic conflict. The following seem to be amongst the most important:

(1) The marginalization of minorities who attempt to maintain their traditional culture even when they are put into reservations which provide an inadequate basis for that culture.

(2) The exploitation of unfree labour, whether in the form of slavery, indentures or the servile labour of peasants.

(3) The maintenance of social distance between rulers and ruled which occurs even where there is no exploitation of unfree labour (e.g. the arrogant self-assurance of the administrative caste in India).

(4) The occurrence of secondary colonialism in the form of pariah trade.

(5) Competition for jobs and other resources between settlers and natives.

(6) The maintenance of social order in the absence of a legal basis in an estate system.

(7) The revolt of colonial peoples against metropolitan domination seen as distinct from the revolt of workers against their capitalist masters.

In situations like these lie the sources of modern race relations situations. Not only do they exist in colonial societies themselves, but they are projected into the metropolis itself. This will form the topic of our next chapter.

In placing the emphasis on colonial society we run the risk of being dubbed proponents of the '"1492" school of race relations': of holding that all problems of racial and ethnic conflict arose as a result of European expansion and colonization. Certainly we have

emphasized the structural origins of these conflicts in colonial institutions. It so happens that much of our experience of these has
been as a result of the '1492' expansion. But the institutions to
which we refer are universal. They existed in the ancient empires of
the Mediterranean and in other empires, and it is right that we
should emphasize them in the general sociology of racial and ethnic
conflict.

Chapter 4

Class, Race and Ethnicity in the Metropolis

In the latter part of the last chapter, attention was focused on the process of modernization of colonial economies and societies. By modernization I mean the supersession of the institutions of 'booty capitalism' by those of western capitalism peacefully oriented to market opportunities. The theme of this chapter will be what happens where immigrants from outside—especially, but not solely, from colonial territories—seek to enter an established modern capitalist society. I shall consider two models of such developents. The first is that which broadly represents the experience of the United States, the second that of Britain.

The United States of America represents not one society but two. One was the colonial society of the Deep South, the other the settler society of the Northern cities in which the freest development of capitalism hitherto seen in the world was uninhibited by feudal survivals. Our concern here will be not with the society as a whole, but with a settler capitalist society entered by immigrants both from Europe and the 'colonial' Deep South.

For many years there was a society of virtually limitless opportunity. Once the native peoples had been driven back into reservations, an open frontier made economic opportunities more and more possible for those who started their lives in North America as immigrant workers. Workers in the East who had originally been 'the huddled masses of the poor' needed protection only during the initial stages of their settlement. Thereafter they achieved social mobility either by going West or by seizing the opportunities of entrepreneurship. As they left they would be succeeded by another wave of immigrants who could be exploited as ruthlessly as they had been.

Obviously such a process eventually reached its end, but for many years the so-called American Dream was a reality and shaped the social institutions of the society. Characteristically this was a capitalist society that had found a way of avoiding class struggle. The trade union movement was weak and had little political expression in the form of a popular workers' party.

There was, of course, class struggle of a bitter kind in particular factories and localities. It could hardly be otherwise where labour was so cheap. But the unit of worker organization was as much as anything the immigrant association. It was to his fellow ethnics that the workers looked for protection, and, so far as the political system was concerned, it was the immigrant community, through the precinct boss, that traded its votes for political favours.

Ethnicity under this system was a powerful resource, used for purposes of industrial and political class struggle. Most Americans began their lives in the United States as hyphenated Americans, i.e. as Irish Americans, Italian Americans, and ethnicity was a factor in the lives of the majority of workers in a way in which it never was in European countries. Yet, important though it was, it did not prevent entry into mainstream society. In three or four generations the descendants of immigrants were fully Americanized and remembered their folk culture only ritually on special occasions. They did not see themselves as a separate culture and society struggling against that of the mainstream.

There were, however, limits to the process of absorption. While one European group after another was assimilated, there seemed to be far more difficulty in assimilating or absorbing the descendants of Black slaves, the native American people, Mexicans, Orientals and Latin Americans.

Blacks followed the European immigrants to the Northern cities and competed for the same jobs. However, they obtained the worst-paid and least acceptable jobs only, and many remained unemployed. It has been said that the real tragedy of the North American Blacks was not that they were subject to ultra-exploitation, but that they were not exploited at all. Segregated residentially, they were left in ghettoes to rot. After several generations many of them lived in a culture of unemployment.

Viewing their situation in 1964, Gunar Myrdal suggested that they could only be described as an underclass. He considered it was the only suitable term to describe the situation of the

unemployed and gradually unemployable persons and families at the bottom of a society in which, for the majority of people above the level, the increasingly democratic structure of the educational system creates more and more liberty .... at least over the course of the generations.

(Myrdal 1964)

So far as other minorities were concerned, the so-called Indians were caught between two worlds. On the one hand, they did not wish to give up their own social institutions and culture even if assimilation were offered to them. On the other, the reserves denied them the facilities necessary for those institutions to operate. They remained outside of the society, living often in conditions of squalor and despair.

The Mexicans, coming as they did from a neighbouring territory, were in a position to maintain their culture through direct contact with their own society. They were not seen, moreover, as having the same rights to be in the United States as European immigrants. For a long period it seemed they were likely to be the most disadvantaged of all immigrants, not left out of the economy like the Blacks, but subject to ultra-exploitation, the more so if their legal status as immigrants was in question.

Similar conditions faced the later immigrants from Latin America, except that their condition was likely to be the more wretched in that they did not have the same access to their homeland as the Mexicans. Black Puerto Ricans and Haitians suffered particularly because the disadvantage of Blackness was added to that of being Latins.

Finally, there were the Orientals, including Japanese, Chinese and Koreans, who came to seek employment and economic opportunity, and the Vietnamese who came as refugees after the end of the Vietnam war. They were able to find economic niches in which they could pursue profits and they were often successful as middlemen (Bonacich 1973). It is still unclear, however, whether they will become a successful part of the capitalist mainstream.

All in all, what we see in the case of the United States is a society as open as any has ever been to social mobility. Ethnicity plays a powerful part because it is a society of immigrants, but what ethnicity does is give protection to new settlers until they can make the grade as individuals who no longer need the support of solidary organizations. This open society system appears, however, to be closed to certain groups, most especially to Black Americans who have been largely denied the opportunity—except recently by the artificial method of affirmative action by governments—of attaining individual security. The biggest divide of all in American society is racial. Blacks are still thought of by many White Americans as outsiders and are increasingly conscious that they have to take collective action with their fellow Blacks if they are to gain rights of entry to the society. The Black urban riots of the 1960s gave reason to doubt whether they would ever succeed in doing so and gain acceptance as equal Americans.

We have discussed the United States case here as though it were a metropolitan society, which, of course, strictly speaking it is not. It is a country without a native-born working class, so the major confrontation of groups takes place between two kinds of immigrants. Unlike the metropolitan countries, it had within itself an open frontier with all the opportunities for mobility that implies. To understand the problems of race in the metropolis, therefore, we would do well to look at Britain which has its own class structure independent of the question of immigrant labour, and where there is no equivalent, except in the Empire itself, of the Open Frontier or the American Dream.

Britain is the society par excellence that exhibits the social structural problems of capitalism. It was also the society in which Marx developed the sociological model of the capitalist system.

The major Marxian hypothesis about capitalist society relates to the rise of the proletariat within bourgeois capitalist society and its eventual achievement of hegemony and the ushering in of a new social order. Ironically using the Hegelian notions of things-in-themselves becoming things-for-themselves, Marx refers to the rise of the working class in these terms in his *Poverty of Philosophy* (1962d):

> Economic conditions had first transformed the mass of the people of the country into workers. The combination of capital has created for this mass a common situation, common interests. The mass is thus already a class against capital, but not yet for itself. In the struggle of which we have noted only a few phases, this mass becomes united, and constitutes itself as a class-for-itself. The interest it defends become class interests. But the struggle of class against class is a political struggle.

Leaving aside the irony, however, Marx presents us (Figure 5) with a sociological problem. There is a stage in the development of capitalist society in which the working class may be thought of as what Marx calls a class in itself, but, as history progresses, he believes that this working class will become a class-for-itself. What *sociological* meaning can be given to these notions?

Marx's answer is given in 'The Communist Manifesto' (Marx and Engels 1962a) which he and Engels wrote when they were addressing practical political problems the year after the *Poverty of Philosophy* was published. They outline the structural stages in the development of the bourgeoisie in its rise to hegemony, then say of the proletariat's rise that 'a similar movement is going on before our very eyes'. If that were the case, the following elements would appear to be involved:

(1) The workers would become conscious of their shared interests and would see those interests as in conflict with those of their employers.

(2) They would form groups of an associational kind (i.e. trades unions) to further their interests.

(3) Many local groups would come together to form a national organization.

(4) The struggle with employers in the collective bargaining which arises in the labour market would lead to organizations on the political level to oppose the political forces supporting the employers.

(5) The associations of the workers and their political parties would generate amongst the vast majority of workers a communal consciousness and a sense of identification with their class, which was stronger than any other identification (e.g. with the nation).

(6) The political party of the workers would not merely negotiate better terms of existence with that of the bourgeoisie but would seek to overthrow its rule. A new social and economic order would be established in which the aims of the proletariat would be realized.

It is not clear what the proletarian goals would be in a society marked by the dictatorship of the proletariat (a term which Marx used first in 1851, in his 'Address to the Communist League') (1962b), since what we know empirically of these goals arises from our experience of the proletariat acting defensively or in conflict rather than in a situation in which it rules. Marx, however, had indicated in his earlier writing that he did not regard the proletariat's achievement of hegemony as simply the rise to power of another class that would pursue its own interests, but rather a class that would stand for the interests of all mankind. Thus in the 'Critique of the Hegelian Philosophy of Right' (Marx 1967) he had spoken of

> a class which is the dissolution of all classes, a sphere of society which has a universal character because its sufferings are universal and which does not claim a particular redress, because the wrong which is done to it is not a particular wrong, but wrong in general.

We may perhaps be justified in listing this as Marx's seventh assumption about the rise to power of the proletariat.

The purpose of this excursus into Marxian philosophy and sociology is not, however, simply to affirm it as true. What we are aiming at is an account of the normal structure of British capitalist society in order better to understand the structural problems generated by the coming of colonial and other immigrants. The Marxian propositions as set out above simply have the merit of clarity. We now need to revise them in a way that makes sense of a century and a half of subsequent political experience. It is this revised picture that will enable us to understand the structural responses of this society to incoming immigrants.

Unlike a population that shares a common ethnicity, the workers as a class-in-itself are not in the first place even a quasi-group or community (i.e. a population with a shared feeling of belonging together within which groups might be created). The class-in-itself has no bond of union other than its common interests: the ways in which its members must act, given the constraints facing them, to achieve their goals. The very notion of class-in-itself is designed to assert that the mere possession of such interests through facing the same constraints does not of itself excite a communal feeling of belonging together. Such a communal feeling is likely to emerge only after *associative* action has been taken.

It may be asked at this point whether there now is a pure 'class-in-itself' in this sense. Clearly at local level those who work together live together in communities, and at this level there must be communal ties and feelings associated with the sharing of common interests. Such communal ties, however, are not helpful in the formation of the 'class-in-itself' in two respects: they will involve communal ties of a deferential kind with the employing class and they are deeply tied in particular to locality rather than to a nationwide experience.

The difficulty about the creation of a 'class-for-itself' is that it requires an orientation on the part of individuals which is at odds with all ties which are in any sense primordial. The new consciousness and new ties have to be found on the basis of a rationalistic argument, which runs: 'I have a particular interest which is similar to that of A, B, and C etc., but which is in conflict with that of X, Y and Z. I therefore wish to organize with A, B and C to realize my goals in accordance with my interests.' The occurrence of such an argument in the minds of many actors itself requires a considerable degree of rationality and a political consciousness strong enough to transcend primordial ties of any sort. Moreover, if it is difficult for workers in a single factory to achieve such a conscious-

ness, it is the more difficult to imagine the fulfilment of conditions
(3), (4) and (5) above, that is to say projecting organization from
the industrial to the political and from the regional to the national
level, as well as developing a communal type of identification with
the national organization.

To this micro-sociological scepticism a committed practical
Marxist in Britain might well reply that there is nonetheless in
Britain a belief by many workers in the existence of a working-class
movement on the industrial and political level to which they are
deeply attached in a communal way. It might even be argued that
the ties which many people feel to this movement transcend any ties
with local community, the nation or any other social object.
Common suffering, the experience of industrial conflicts, and participation in parliamentary and extra-parliamentary political action
have given rise to this feeling. That is why half of the electorate
have supported the Labour Party over a long period. An equivalent
development, it will be argued, has occurred in other European
countries.

Clearly there is some truth in this. But it must also be recognized
that the experience of local community and the experience of
patriotism generated by wars pull against such working-class identification. That is why working-class political consciousness is
subverted by such things as wars and football matches (football
teams usually being powerful foci of local allegiance). Sorel (1961)
grasped a very important truth when he saw that working-class
unity required a powerful myth like that of the general strike to
counter all this.

It we allow, however, that such mythology does exist and does
produce a sense of communal identification and common struggle
at least in a good number of individuals, the real problems with the
Marxian sociology of class arise in relation to point (6) and the
seventh point which we have added about the universal class.

One thing that does happen and might be expected as a strong
possibility, given our argument in Chapter 1, is that when collective
bargaining occurs either on the individual or on the political level,
the working class, even it if is deemed to exist both associatively
and communally, might very well strike a bargain with its oppon-
ents. Moreover, given that we have no instance of proletarian
hegemony occurring in a developed capitalist society, it must be
assumed either that the proletariat has been defeated or that such
a bargain has been struck.

A number of writers (Lipset 1960, Marshall 1950, Dahrendorf
1957, Rex 1967) have suggested that some such bargain typically
occurs in capitalist societies which have previously been marked by

class struggle. The following points, it is suggested, have been agreed by Labour and Capital on a political level and form the foundation of what is called in a wide sense the Welfare State:

(1) That workers shall have the freedom to engage in collective bargaining over their wages and conditions.

(2) That the government shall take responsibility for planning the economy in such a way that nearly full-employment is achieved.

(3) That the best way of achieving this is through a mixed economy, so that both total free enterprise and total collective ownership are ruled out.

(4) That workers in times of unemployment, ill-health and retirement will be entitled to a basic income paid for on the basis of compulsory insurance contributions by employers and workers.

(5) That all people will be entitled to a basic standard of health, housing, education and other personal social services, the cost of which will be borne partly by general taxation.

It will readily be objected that this outcome does not occur in all capitalist societies at all times. Clearly it does not occur in the United States in the form outlined, and political developments in the 1980s in Britain suggest that the Welfare State deal has been abandoned there. This, however, does not refute the argument. What is being suggested is that the five points outlined are the *most* that will be achieved by class struggle. If we are concerned with the relation of ethnic minorities to the class structure, the existence of this Welfare State deal is the polar possibility along the road of working-class influence in politics. We should also consider what happens when the working class are prevented from realizing all of these conditions (as in Britain in the 1980s). What is far less relevant to any modern industrial society is to seek to understand the problems of immigrants in relation to a working class which is heading for hegemony based upon the collective ownership of the major means of production, distribution and exchange. That is to say a realistic prediction of workers' behaviour (*inter alia* towards immigrants) would have to assume workers were embarked upon an attempt to sustain the Welfare State as outlined. It could not be based upon the assumption of a working class consciously heading for hegemony.

Marxists might well argue that the forms of consciousness we are suggesting are the only ones likely to be sustained in the light of the kind of economic crisis which Marx envisages in the 'Preface to the Critique of Political Economy' (1962a), when the existing social relations of production 'become a fetter on production' or when the kinds of economic difficulties envisaged in *Capital* ensue. To this we might reply that economists have yet to be convinced of

Marx's labour theory of value, which is at the heart of his economics, and that, in any case, the expected insurmountable crisis of capitalism has not ensued in more than a century since he wrote. Even if Marxian economic predictions were held to be valid, it would still have to be shown that they were believed in by substantial sections of the working class before it became hegemonic. In Gramscian terms, the working classes we have known are corporate rather than hegemonic.

Nothing that has been said above should lead one to conclude that the population at large might not have profoundly different attitudes towards immigrant and other minorities in a command economy: we should keep an open mind on this until adequate evidence has been assembled. In question is simply the belief that a society like that in Britain is embarked upon an inevitable movement towards proletarian hegemony and socialism.

What then is the structural position of immigrant workers entering this political system likely to be? We must now seek to answer this question by first assuming the existence of the set of institutional arrangements described above as the Welfare State, then assuming that the consensus they envisage has been abandoned by the ruling or entrepreneurial class.

It is of some importance here to consider the different meaning which the term 'underclass' would have in the kind of society which we are envisaging as existing in Britain compared with its meaning in the United States. There, according to Myrdal, the underclass consists of those who have failed to become economically self-supporting, i.e. to become individuals in an open, status-seeking society. In the British case, where politics are based much more upon the notion of collective action in support of interests, rather than on individual competitiveness, the crucial distinction is between those who do and those who don't share in the 'Welfare State deal'. As I have written elsewhere.

> In using the term (underclass) here we use it in a different sense because (a) the normal social pattern which we assume is not that of 'liberty' so much as welfare guaranteed by class politics and (b) what we want to point to is the situation of immigrant minorities, who do not share in this welfare deal, but who, instead of forming an inert or despairing social residue, organize and act in their own 'underclass' interest often relating themselves to colonial class positions.
>   (Rex and Tomlinson 1979, p. 328)

It should now be noted that a 'Welfare State deal' makes some differences to the very nature of the class structure. The Marxist view is that class membership arises from the individual's relation to the means of production. But if it is true, as Marshall suggests, that under the Welfare State the individual has acquired social rights on top of his legal and political rights, and that his allegiance to the nation-state is therefore stronger than his allegiance to class, then the only continuing meaning that class can have is in the rights which he has acquired. According to the account given here, these rights include not only the right to use industrial power, but also the right to a job, to an income when out of a job and to a basic standard of health care, housing, education and personal social services. Some would go further in the direction of revisionism by denying that collective bargining was either a necessary right or consistent with the other rights mentioned.

In any case, it is clear that an individual's position and rights in the Welfare State turn, apart from the membership of a free trade union, on access to employment, social insurance, health, housing, education and personal social services. Weber, it will be remembered, suggested that class situation depended upon market situation and that wherever there was a difference in the distribution of property there was a market and hence classes. Taking this only a stage further we may say that wherever there is a system of allocation of scarce resources of any kind there will be classes. This Weberian revision of Marxism suggests therefore that under the 'Welfare State deal' the position of the working class is defined in terms of certain social rights, and that whether or not any minority group is part of the working class depends upon whether it shares fully in these rights.

Before going on to consider the position of immigrant minorities, we should note that assimilation and acceptance into a capitalist society has a different meaning under the American model and under the British Welfare State model. Under the former, an individual is assimilated and accepted when he is capable of standing on his own feet as a property-owning individual. Under the latter, it will depend upon his acceptance into a working class which itself possesses considerable social rights.

This is not the place to answer the empirical questions of whether or not various immigrant minorities in Britain or in Europe actually enjoy the rights of the incorporated working class. What can be done here is to specify the questions which would have to be asked to determine whether this is so. These questions include the following:

(1) Does the minority group member share in the right to collective bargaining over his wages and conditions or does the native working class exercise a monopoly over these rights? In other

words, are the minority members of trades unions and do they enjoy the effective support of trades unions?

(2) Do the minority members enjoy equal access to employment in a range of different jobs if they are qualified and are they able to gain promotion? Are their jobs segregated?

(3) Are minority members more liable to unemployment?

(4) Do minority members have equal access to housing of differing degrees of desirability and are they segregated in the housing which they do acquire?

(5) Do minority members have equal access to education and equal chances of getting through the various selection mechanisms which form part of the educational system? To what extent do they receive education in their own values and culture and in that of the main society?

(6) Do minority members have equal protection before the law and is their experience of police the same?

The detailed specification of these questions will enable us to find out how far a minority has gained full rights in the society or how far it has become an 'underclass' (in the special sense in which that term may be used in the British Welfare State model).

The first question concerns both participants in trades unions and the service which minorities receive from unions. These are, in fact, two distinct questions. Minorities may join unions and actively participate in them, but not find the unions acting in their interests because of their lack of control of executive bodies.

Participation in trades unions rarely replaces the strong communal feelings ethnic minorities have towards their fellow ethnics. The unions represent a kind of associative activity which may well cross-cut but neither supports nor replaces ethnic ties. In addition to the unions themselves, however, ethnic communities may form unions within unions to safeguard their special interests. Such unions within unions are groups formed within the quasi-group and express communal feelings as well as being rational associations. In the alternative American model above, trades unions themselves have been shaped by these ethnic organizations and sometimes they even operate without trades unions.

In fact, it is difficult for ethnic working-class leaders to maintain the allegiance of their fellow ethnics to formal trades unions, the more so because within such associations the native-born leadership often fights to defend the interests of native-born workers to the exclusion of all competitors. The ethnic minority trades unionist may well find, therefore, that he is a member of an association which not only fails to represent his interests, but actually works against them.

So far as obtaining jobs is concerned, whether the minority worker is opposed in seeking employment or not will depend upon whether he is seeking the same jobs. The dual labour market thesis (Doeringer and Piore 1971) states that there are two distinct labour markets, and that it is possible for two kinds of workers not to be in competition with each other at all. This extreme situation rarely exists in reality, but it may well be true that there are classes of jobs whose low wages, unpleasant working conditions and insecurity make them unattractive to natives whose educational system has led them to aspire to white collar and skilled jobs, and the jobs are therefore open to any applicant. Statistically, minorities may be concentrated in these less desirable jobs and it is precisely these jobs that native-led unions fail to service and protect.

Much more difficult than the absorption of minority workers into some kind of employment is their promotion to skilled and supervisory work. It is quite possible that unions will accept the employment of minorities in low-grade jobs, but resist the demands of these workers to enter the more rewarding jobs. Here a *de facto* colour bar might operate.

Finally, there is the question of the experience of unemployment. In times of prosperity, unemployment rates amongst minority workers will approximate that of natives, once the initial difficulties of immigration have been overcome, but if the minorities have not become integrated and lack control over the unions, when unemployment rises minority employees are more at risk and their unemployment rate is likely to rise more sharply than that of the natives.

Behind the question of employment lies the question of immigration control. If immigration law makes it difficult for certain categories of workers to immigrate legally, then there will be illegal immigration and even those who have the necessary legal documents to claim their rights will be under pressure. This will affect not only the right to such work, but, perhaps more importantly, the right to claim social insurance benefits, which involves direct contact with the state.

The fourth question concerns housing problems which are equivalent and yet distinct areas. In an early work I wrote,

> There is a class struggle over the use of houses and thus class struggle
> is the central process of the city as a social unit.
>
> (Rex and Moore 1967)

My suggestion was that the differential access which individuals had to desirable housing divided men into housing classes. Interests in the housing system divided the population into housing-classes-in-themselves and urban politics was likely to be as much as anything the arena of housing-class struggle on a class-for-itself basis. Of course the specific type of housing-class-struggle would depend upon what housing stock was available and on the values of different sections of the population, but clearly it would be true that in any case interest would conflict. The native community might have values V and therefore seek certain types of housing while the incoming minority might have values W which lead to their seeking other types of housing. Such demands on the system might be complementary (i.e. there might be a dual housing market), but in conditions of severe housing shortage they are likely to conflict.

One important consequence of housing-class-struggle is residential segregation. Insofar as minority people are forced to live together, communal ethnic ties will be strengthened by daily interaction. Even if the minority workers were to form alliances with their white peers in the workplace, such unity would not be fostered by residential community life, as was the unity of the workers in traditional working-class communities whose neighbourhood life served to reinforce ties at work. Generally, residential segregation is a powerful force against class integration. It fosters instead the *de facto* differential incorporation of the minority workers who are seen to belong to separate communities.

Insofar as education may be thought of as a scarce resource capable of being differentially allocated, one might be inclined to speak of education classes equivalent to housing classes. There are difficulties about this in that schools not merely give the scarce good 'education' to differing types of individuals in differing degrees, but are also the means whereby all individuals, including immigrants, are socialized into the society of settlement, so that some things might be denied but there are other things which schools insist on giving to all their pupils indiscriminately. It will be useful to look at both of these aspects of education separately.

So far as selection is concerned, different countries have different systems. The British system is a severely competitive one with several different kinds of education and therefore different types of passport to occupational success on offer. There is a fee-paying sector; there has been and still is a tripartite division into different types of education within the free state sector; and there are some schools which have better reputations than others. What happens to minority children will depend upon whether they can afford the fee-paying sector and be admitted if they seek to enter it, and on how far the various selection processes which lead to children being assigned to schools with desirable types of syllabus and desirable reputations are fair or not. Evidence from both the United States and Britain suggests that minority children are placed overwhelmingly in the worst sections of the worst schools. Indeed, native parents come to regard the presence of minority children as an indication that the schooling on offer is inferior. It is fair to say, therefore, that there are education classes and that minorities tend to be placed in the most disadvantaged classes.

Turning to the socializing as distinct from the selection aspect of education, schools must have the effect of undermining the values system and the social solidarity of minorities by indoctrinating them with the host society's values. This creates an apparent dilemma for minority parents. Should they insist upon education in their own values and thereby allow their children to receive differentiated and possibly inferior treatment? Or should they accept what education has to offer by way of improving their children's life-chances at the expense of their losing their own culture? The dilemma is only resolved if it is recognized that a modern industrial society has a common culture of the public domain which the schools should inculcate, and which represents no threat to the folk-culture of the minorities which can be maintained and respected in the private domain. In fact, the decision to offer special syllabuses to minorities would usually work to their disadvantage, even though such offerings might be justified on grounds of respect for minority culture. The problem for a minority is to find ways of fostering their own culture, probably outside the school, while at the same time insisting on equal treatment in the school, particularly if it equips children for occupational success.

The seal would be set on the incorporation of minorities in a society by the fact that they were equal before the law. *Per contra*, nothing indicates more sharply the extent of differential incorporation than differential treatment by the police.

Police in any society exercize the awesome responsibility of having a monopoly of the right to use physical violence legitimately. The question is how far they use that right to protect society and all its citizens or how far they exercize it on behalf of some special interest. They may harass particular communities, they may take sides in disputes or they may fail to intervene to stop attacks by one group upon another. If they do any of these things, the right is being used in effect to outlaw a particular section or to demonstrate its differential incorporation.

What has been said above, it must be pointed out again, is not intended as a description of British society or any other. It is an agenda of questions which must be asked if we are to decide whether or not an immigrant minority is being forced into the position of an underclass. The answer to the empirical question of what actually occurs on these points is given for Britain by David Smith's authoritative *Racial Disadvantage in Britain* (1967), based on national survey evidence, and my book with Sally Tomlinson, *Colonial Immigrants in a British City* (1979). This evidence shows that there is no total and complete separation of immigrant minorities on a class-basis. Some do obtain desirable jobs, stay out of unemployment, get good suburban housing and good education for their children, as well as enjoying the protection of the police. But statistically speaking the chances of a family not enjoying these rights are overwhelmingly greater for immigrant minorities than they are for the host community. It is this majority who form the immigrant underclass.

We should note here that what we have said assumes the existence of the 'Welfare State deal'. If, however, the Welfare State is abandoned in a situation of recession, as to some extent has happened in Britain in the 1980s, it will be more difficult to make the distinctions between working class and underclass because many native workers will be placed in a position which is in some respects similar to that of the minority underclass.

In this situation, there is the likely development of racist theories by the ruling class as a means of diverting the hostility of unemployed native workers, and the more spontaneous scapegoating by some of these workers who blame the minority for their condition. On the other hand, a strong ruling class may not need scapegoating in these circumstances because it is fully prepared to engaged in open class-war against its own working class. Which of these lines of development was likely to prevail was not yet clear in Britain in the early 1980s. There had been some development of scapegoating both in the form of the development of racist policies by governments and in the form of spontaneous attacks by working-class youth on minority members. But the confrontation between government and striking workers in 1984 and 1985 overshadowed these developments.

Two important variables affecting the emergence of an underclass are the closeness of the minority culture to that of the host society and the length of stay. Thus there does seem to be an important difference between most European immigrant situations and that which prevails in Britain. In North-West Europe, many of the immigrants are from Southern European countries, whose culture has much in common with the countries of settlement. But Turks in Germany and Algerians and Moroccans in France, Belguim and the Netherlands share many of the problems of the immigrants _om South Asia, the Caribbean and Africa who are the most visible immigrants in Britain. Tentatively we may suggest that the situation of Southern Europeans in North-West Europe is one of immigration only, while that of the Turks, North Africans, Asians and West Indians is one of immigration *and* race relations. Immigrant communities may expect to see their descendants absorbed into the host society and culture in three or four generations. The prospects for the more geographically and culturally distant migrants and especially racially distinguishable migrants are less hopeful. They may well remain distinct for a much longer period or may stay as a culturally disorganized but deprived underclass of a more permanent kind.

This is not, of course, to say that immigrants as such do not have problems. They do, and for the period before their absorption they are subject to racial discrimination and racism. (Even though they are racially the same as the natives they will be held to be racially different.) Ties of kinship are strained by immigration and an alternative organization based on new immigrant associations is necessary to sustain them during this period. Such immigrant associations are in effect places of sanctuary, organizations for pastoral care, the means of affirming and sustaining the minority culture, as well as organizations for defending their interest (see Rex 1973). But they also constitute a springboard from which children and grandchildren succeed in entering the host society as full members. Provision for their needs is gradually passed from the immigrant associations to the organizations of the active working class or those of the state.

By contrast with this picture, the more distant and distinct minorities may stay permanently in a segregated minority position. They will retain their own languages and religion and will try to impose a rule of endogamy on their children. Extended kinship will remain strong and the extended kin-group will serve as a means of mobilizing financial and other capital with a view to achieving self-sufficiency.

Thus far we have suggested that the common fate of immigrants, whether for two or three generations or more permanently, will be that of an underclass, that is, of a quasi-group with a distinct class position and status weaker and lower than that of the working class. But the very segregation of communities helps, as the previous paragraph suggests, the mobilization of resources and that is bound to have some measure of success. This leads me at least to suggest that along with the underclass model we need another which recognizes such success. I shall call it the separate pyramid model.

Historically, Jewish refugee communities in Britain and elsewhere and more recently South Asian communities in Britain have approximated to the separate pyramid model. In the case of the Asians, the basis of this had been complex. The immigrants from India and Pakistan and East Africa came from very varied backgrounds. There were early immigrants connected with the cotton trade as merchants, and others from India and East Africa who came if not as businessmen, at least with business skills. Along with them came some poor migrants following in the wake of runaway seamen and peddlers, but also better-off peasants who came to earn money so that they could improve their status as landowners.

Both members of the migrating business communities and other poor immigrants saw Britain as a land of economic opportunity. Wages available were high compared with incomes available in India, especially for those who live frugally and worked night-shifts and overtime, and for those who saved money there were occupational niches they could fill as entrepreneurs. Thus in the second generation, even though the majority may still have been factory workers, there was a thriving 'Indian' economy, involving not merely shop-keeping but wholesaling, manufacture and tertiary enterprises of all kinds.

Business success was accompanied by the scholastic success of school-children. The schools offered a way to further business success and also to enter the professions. Children were encouraged to learn all that they could so that their knowledge could be used for economic advancement. Very soon it became apparent that Asian children were actually doing as well or better at school than English children. Apparently the combination of a strong culturally based home background and an instrumental attitude towards education was a recipe for success.

What has been said above represents something of an exaggeration. But that is true of all ideal types. Provided we are not deceived by the *stereotype* of the successful Indians to believe that all Indians are successful, it is useful for analytic purposes. What we now have to notice is that, however successful South Asians might be in business and the professions, this does not mean that they necessarily fully enter English business and the professions. Segregation confines them in a separate pyramid.

We should not exaggerate the extent of this segregation and suggest that it is total. Total segregation would mean that Asians traded with and employed only Asians. It is true they trade more with Asians and employ other Asians, especially in their businesses, but there is some interaction between the two economies.

Diagrammatically we may express the position of such a community as in Figure 8.

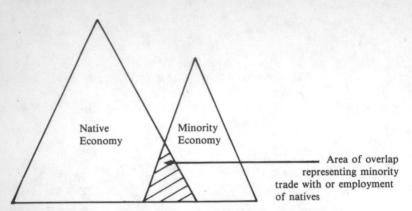

Figure 8. *Relation of native and immigrant minority economies*

The minority pyramid is much narrower than the native one, but might reach nearly as high.

One may expect that if this economy continues to grow, there will be an increasing area of overlap and the beginnings of contact on a class basis, not only amongst the workers, but amongst the rich and the employers (Figure 9).

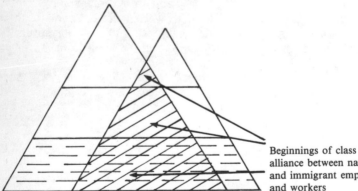

Figure 9. *Future development of native and immigrant economies*

There are, however, factors making against this development, which if taken to its conclusion would lead to the replacement of the two pyramids by a division cross-cutting the two economies on class-lines. Particularly, they turn on the notions of pariahs and scapegoating.

Pariah activities are economic and social activities necessary to a society, yet deemed undesirable. Pariah people are, therefore, both encouraged to perform the activities and punished for doing so. To some extent, the immigrant economy will be forced to remain centred around activities of this kind which will prevent its assimilation to the mainstream.

Secondly, there is the question of scapegoating. The whole of the economy is precarious and subject to economic disaster. It also involves exploitation and class struggle. It is convenient, therefore, to have an ideology which places the blame for these dangers away from those in charge. The Indian entrepreneur provides the scapegoat in just this way.

An interesting, more specific, example is derived from my own research experience in Birmingham (Rex and Moore 1967). There the housing system had failed many people including, but not entirely consisting of, immigrants. Pakistani landlords converted houses to lodging-houses and provided accommodation for those who were not otherwise provided for. In so doing, they were providing an essential service which the city took for granted. That, however, did not prevent the authorities from arraigning the landlords before the courts and blaming them for the evil conditions. The trial of these landlords was essentially a ritual in which pariahs were serving as scapegoats.

Envy of the economically successful immigrant minority coupled with racism might lead to another type of scapegoating on a more popular political level. Political organizations arise to demonstrate against such communities through street marches, and the police may turn a relatively blind eye to other more informal physical attacks. The demand is then made on a political level for the 'repatriation' of the minority or any other way of getting rid of them. Against this background it is by no means certain that the immigrant society and economy will undergo the simple process of change envisaged in Figures 8 and 9.

We are now in a position to consider what will happen in a society in which a racially distinguishable minority or some other minority does not undergo a process of assimilation. We suggest that it will either form an underclass, in the sense of that term used here, or that it will form a separate social and economic pyramid. What factors will tell against this? Basically there are two. On the one hand, there will be a response from the disadvantaged and segregated minorities. On the other, there may be some attempt to modify the position by governments and political parties with more universalistic values.

Acquiescence in an underclass position is only likely to make their position permanent, so it is to be expected that the ethnic minorities will set up their own organizations for purposes of collective bargaining. An example of this was the National Association for the Advancement of the Coloured People in the United States, but such organizations are not easy to set up if other organizations already exist. In particular, the already available organizations will include those which are oriented to the politics of the homeland, to larger and more diffuse cultural issues or towards collaborative activity with working-class organizations. Thus in Britain, Sikhs organize on behalf of their fellow-Sikhs in the Punjab, and Greek-Cypriots are concerned with the Cyprus issue: there are many cultural organizations concerned with fostering traditional culture or, as amongst the West Indians, in creating a new one based on Black Consciousness; and there are organizations like the Marxist Indian Workers Association which are concerned with the position of Indian workers as workers. All of these tendencies, important though they may be in their own right, are pressures against the formation of organizations specifically concerned with breaking down the barriers which serve to segregate and disadvantage the minority community. Nonetheless it is to be expected that such specific collective bargaining organizations will develop in the future.

Governments in the democracies are always to some extent motivated by universalistic values, and this is particularly true in the United States where the Supreme Court acts, albeit imperfectly, as the guardian of such values. There is, therefore, likely to emerge in such a society some kind of critique of racism and racial discrimination. More than this, the consequence of the acceptance of the theory of the Black underclass has been that the state has intervened in order forcibly to encourage examples of minority success and assimilation. Such American policies have had their imitators elsewhere. We shall deal with the problems which such policies involve in Chapters 6 and 7. Before this, however, for completeness we should say something about situations in which ethnicity does not necessarily lead to macro-political problems of the kind we have been discussing.

Chapter 5

Benign and Malign Ethnicity

Theories of Ethnicity

In the first and second chapters, it was suggested that there was some doubt as to whether ethnic and race relations constituted a field of study in its own right. The focus was on the relations between ethnic and racial quasi-groups, but it was argued that these were normally the relations dealt with by sociologists in their study of class and estate systems (or, as most sociologists would say, stratification systems). The main significance of race and ethnicity is that it provided the basis for social bonding within the quasi-groups.

In the third and fourth chapters, attention was paid to systems marked by 'conflict, discrimination, oppression and exploitation', and it was shown that many situations seen as race relations situations, as well as some which were purely ethnic, whether in colonial societies or amongst immigrants in the metropolis, were of this kind. Indeed, it was because they were of this kind that they gave rise to problems worthy of intellectual attention. There is, however, another view, namely that the field of race and ethnicity need not necessarily be confined to the sociology of conflict, and that there are important sociological problems even when groups are in a state of mutual dependency and cooperation. This seems to be the view of many anthropologists, particularly those who have developed from the several writings of Frederick Barth.

Barth's own exposition of his theory of ethnic boundary processes is by no means easy to follow, particularly as his arguments are not directed against the positions expounded here, but against those adopted by other anthropologists. Before we set them out, therefore, it will be useful to recall the position we have reached here in order to compare it with that of Barth and his followers.

The position set out in the previous chapters is that what we called ethnic and racial 'quasi-groups' were brought together in situations of conflict. We now have to spell this out more clearly in order to compare and contrast it with the theory of ethnicity as expounded by the anthropologists. This will mean looking both at the constitution of the so-called 'quasi-groups' and at the relations between them.

We spoke of quasi-groups because the social entities involved had neither the characteristics of associations nor of communities. They were not in themselves groups, but provided a source from which group life of all kinds, both associative and communal, might emerge. All that existed in the first place was the presence of shared racial or cultural characteristics. We must now ask what it means to speak of shared characteristics in this sense.

The first point is loosely referred to as consciousness of kind. We assumed that it would be normal for human beings as they mapped their world to take account of human features within it which were reminiscent of their own, though we probably also assumed that what was especially important was familiar *behaviour*. Mere similarity of physical features could have some effect in that such features would arouse memories of tender care within the family which would not be aroused to the same degree by dissimilar features. But more important than this would be seeing other people behaving in familiar ways.

Why such familiar forms of behaviour should arouse special feelings is a fundamental and difficult question in sociology. Basically, there are three explanations. The Freudian one is that appropriate forms of behaviour are those which avoid the guilt associated with the Oedipal Story. According to this view, appropriate behaviour is that which is not tabooed and is in opposition to that which is. A second view emerges from Durkheim's *Elementary Forms of Religious Life* (1915), which suggests that there are people, objects and ways of behaving which have a sacred quality because they are associated with collective life. The third view is that of W. G. Sumner, who argued in his *Folkways* (1959) that while the folkways were only morally neutral group habits, they become morally charged when they were seen in opposition to the folkways of others. At this point they appeared sacred. They became mores.

It cannot be said that any of these explanations is wholly convincing, but it can at least be noted that all the authors are agreed that such forms of behaviour are not merely observed as part of a cognitive mapping, but are also regarded as in some sense sacred.

So far, however, we have only spoken of those whose behaviour is *similar* to that of a particular individual. This is actually a very mechanical way of looking at the matter. Some of the behaviour an individual observes is not similar so much as complementary. It is because individuals perform acts which might be thought of as helpful that their behaviour appeals.

Here, of course, we are on the verge of saying that the other individuals interact with us as members of a group, but it is important to recognize that there may be a recognizable potential for helpful action before it actually occurs. This recognition of potentiality helps to constitute the quasi-group.

Against this background we can give more meaning to the notion of communal social relations as existing between members of an ethnic population. The ties we have with other members of our ethnic quasi-group are clearly not valued simply because they might be useful. They are characterized by a feeling of belonging together, of common place and history. As such, they have the semi-sacred qualities referred to above. If this is what it means to say that ethnicity is primordial, we would be bound to agree that it was primordial.

Having ethnic ties in this sense can be seen as an important resource. Any individual looks to his kin and to neighbours as a first resource for cooperative action. Those who are marked and mapped as having similar or complementary behavioural characteristics constitute a secondary resource. We may turn to them when necessary to form groups and to organize collectively for the achievement of goals. This is what it means to say that the ethnic population forms a quasi-group from which group action might emerge, rather than already being a group itself.

Ethnicity is not the only basis for quasi-group formation. The two other main ones are nationality and class. Nationality involves a wider range than ethnicity and also the notion that the other members of the quasi-group are important politically as well as morally. So far as class is concerned, the crux of the matter is that the other individuals are perceived not simply as appearing or behaving similarly (they may not be), but as having common interests. Separate from class in this narrow sense, one might also note here that estates and castes are very like ethnic quasi-groups in that they are marked by a sense of a common way of life amongst their members, but that both are characterized by hierarchical position and one is a legal and the other a religious entity.

Quasi-groups as such are available for mobilization in larger social systems, and ethnic quasi-groups may become part of estate, caste and class systems. This may mean that the ethnic quasi-group is treated like an estate, caste or class within the larger system or it may mean more radically that it has taken on, in addition to those characteristics which arise from ethnicity, the characteristics of an estate, caste or class. Along with other forms of behaviour associated with ethnicity, therefore, fellow ethnics are seen as sharing a position in a caste or estate hierarchy or as having common interests.

The relationship between class and ethnicity is especially interesting. Class starts out as class-in-itself, as a plurality of individuals with unperceived common interests. Those interests are then perceived and seen to be in conflict with those of other classes. The members of the class then form associations, but these associations acquire communal characteristics as time goes on. Eventually the class is far from being a merely associative group, because its members come to have a shared experience of struggle and a sense of the moral and political importance of their fellows' behaviour just as great as in any group which starts out as a community. An ethnic group on the other hand moves from consciousness of kind, through the development of a sense of sacredness and of communal ties, to the development of formal associations with express the interests of the ethnic community. Clearly in any ongoing society such groups must interact. Classes become like ethnic communities. Ethnic communities become classes.

In talking about the relationship between ethnic groups, the approach of the first four chapters of this book has been to emphasize conflict. In talking about class, we went beyond the representation of classes as groups bargaining and entering into agreements in the market place to suggest that especially in colonial circumstances such bargaining processes broke down and led to political conflict. In talking about estate and caste systems too, we emphasized that the apparent consensus about which was superior and which inferior was often imposed by force by the upper estates and castes. There is considerable reason for this emphasis, because most socially and ethnically based estate, caste and class systems are not benign. They do not belong, that is to say, in boxes D, E and F in Figure 1, and the problematic part of race and ethnic relations *is* undoubtedly that which belongs in boxes A, B and C.

Nonetheless, there *are* situations of benign ethnicity and benign relations, markets *do* operate for long periods and the upper castes and estates *are* successful in imposing their values and their social system upon others. It is possible, therefore, while emphasizing the conflict approach, to recognize that the same structures might also be usefully analyzed as established systems. Conflict theory should recognize that conflicts might produce truces operating in terms of agreed values (Rex 1961). Equally, functionalist theory should recognize that the functional order it discusses actually seeks to order 'a veritable powder-keg' of explosive conflicts (Devereux 1961). We should bear this in mind as we turn to anthropological theories of ethnicity.

Barth's Theory of Ethnic Boundary Processes

The anthropological problematic of ethnicity arises from the ending of a period in which ethnology sought to study tribes in isolation. Symbolically speaking, their ideal was a tribe on an island cut off from all outside influence so that its internal social system and culture could be studied in its purity. When, however, they studied more complex political circumstances, such as Barth found in his fieldwork in the North-West Frontier Province in Pakistan (Barth 1959), and still more when they studied ethnicity in cities, there was an obvious problem. Where were the boundaries of the group they were studying and how did such boundaries arise?

As Frederick Barth puts the matter:

> Practically all anthropological reasoning rests on the premise that cultural variation is discontinuous; that there are aggregates of people who essentially share a common culture, and interconnected differences that distinguish each such discrete culture from all others.

But whereas 'the differences between cultures and historic boundaries have been given much attention', 'the constitution of ethnic groups and the nature of the boundaries between them, have not been correspondingly investigated' (Barth 1969, p. 9).

Barth finds in the studies of his colleagues two points of importance:

> First, it is clear that boundaries persist despite a flow of personnel across them. In other words, categorised ethnic distinctions do not depend on an absence of mobility, contact and information, but do entail processes of exclusion and incorporation whereby discrete categories are maintained despite changing participation and membership in the course of life histories.
>
> Secondly, one finds that stable, persisting and often vitally important social relations are maintained across such boundaries and are frequently based precisely on the dichotomized ethnic statuses.
>
> (ibid. p. 9-10)

This criticism directed against other anthropologists may also be seen as a criticism of the position expounded in this book. We have started by assuming discrete quasi-groups, then talked about the relationships between them, largely in terms of class, estate and caste as type of social organization. I would maintain that there is great value in this perspective, but that Barth's observations point towards both a complementary field of study, in which other than class factors affect the relations between groups, and a detailed micro-study of the kinds of social organizations which might in any case prevail.

Barth contrasts his own approach with that developed by Narroll. According to Narroll, the term 'ethnic group' is generally understood in anthropology to refer to a population which

(1) is largely biologically self-perpetuating
(2) shares fundamental cultural values realised in overt unity in cultural forms
(3) makes up a field of communication and interaction
(4) has a membership which identifies itself, and is identified by others as constituting a category distinguishable from other categories of the same order.

(ibid. p. 10)

It may be pointed out that this is fairly close to our own position. Under (1) we too have seen that races may be the basis of ethnic quasi-groups. Under (2) we have defined ethnic quasi-groups as existing amongst people with common culture traits. Under (3) we have emphasized that the existence of complementary behaviour patterns provides a potential for interaction and so far as (4) is concerned, in Chapter 2 we have discussed in some detail the ways in which not only do groups identify themselves and become identified, but also the way in which these identifications might conflict.

According to Barth, classification of 'ethnic groups' in terms of cultural characteristics cannot explain why people showing various cultural traits in different places and different times are still seen as belonging to the same group, as they in fact normally are. It is necessary, therefore, to begin with some conception of the organization of this group and to see the sharing of cultural traits as a consequence of that organization. Barth then goes on:

The critical focus of investigation from this point of view becomes the ethnic boundary of the group, not the cultural stuff which it encloses.

(Ibid. p.15)

That is to say the actual cultural items involved might vary with time and place and those included in the same ethnic group or category remain the same. The boundary is a 'vessel', but it may have varying 'contents', e.g. territoriality, history, language, economic practices, symbols. It may use any one or any part of one of these as a marker and reject others.

On the other hand, the ethnic boundary 'canalizes social life' and entails a complex organization of behaviour and social relations. It distinguishes between those who 'are playing the same game', with whom relations may be expanded, and others who are strangers, with whom there must be 'limitations on shared understandings, differences in criteria for judgement of value and performance and a restriction on interaction to sectors of assumed understanding and mutual interest' (ibid. p. 15).

When members of one ethnic group interact with another, it does not follow that they will become more and more like each other. The essence of Barth's case is that in these situations ethnic 'groups' continue to exist.

> Stable interethnic relations presuppose . . . a structuring of interaction: a set of prescriptions governing situations of contact and allowing for the articulation in some sectors or domains of activity, and a set of proscriptions on social situations preventing interethnic interaction in other sectors, and thus insulating parts of the cultures from confrontation and modification.
>
> (ibid. p. 16)

The sort of situation that would fall under this heading, according to Barth, is referred to by Furnivall as a plural society. The separate groups there each have their own boundaries to organize their domestic and religious lives, but rules of interaction for the market place prevent social interaction in areas such as buying and selling, and proscribe it in other areas such as intermarriage and worshipping together.

However, this is only one case and, for Barth, a simple case. Here economic behaviour is permitted between groups and other forms of behaviour not permitted. Other cases are more subtle, such as the Kula ring in the Trobriands, where trade in high prestige objects defines a sphere within which other forms of economic interaction may go on. In other societies, feudal political relations may be permitted between groups. Sometimes economic behaviour will be centralized, but political behaviour polycentral, and so on. For Barth, these are not all instances of the plural society, but they do seem to illustrate the normal process of boundary marking, which is infinitely various, between groups.

Sometimes 'the distinguishing values connected with ethnic identity are relevant only to a few kinds of activities' and are the basis of only a limited form of social organization. In other cases, such as those referred to as 'the plural society' which are 'complex poly-ethnic systems', there are 'extremely relevant value differences and multiple constraints on status combinations and social participation'. The plural society is the extreme case in which there is a radical and surprising separation of groups which engage in economic activity with one another. In many cases, however, ethnic groups persist even though only narrow areas of interactions are proscribed.

Barth goes on to consider the problem from what he calls the ecological and the demographic perspective. From the former, he suggests that groups might be brought together because they occupy separate niches in the natural environment and, therefore, don't compete with one another, they may have separate political territories with only marginally disputed boundaries or they may perform different and complementary economic roles. In all of these cases, peaceful coexistence is possible even though the situation remains polyethnic. Sometimes there is also the possibility of two groups competing for the same niche, but this is usually only transitory.

It would seem from Barth's account of the ecological perspective that interethnic interaction requires a degree of interdependence and symbiosis: 'In field where there is no complementarity', he tells us, 'there can be no basis for organization on ethnic lines—there will either be no interaction, or interaction without reference to ethnic identity' (ibid. p. 18). Apparently he excludes ethnic conflict from consideration here.

Interethnic cooperation also requires certain numerical limits. Any variation in the size of one group must have effects on the other. Hence there will be ways in which the groups adjust:

> a number of factors other than mortality and fertility effect the balance of numbers .... emigration that relieves pressure, immigration that maintains one or several co-resident groups as outpost settlements of larger population reservoirs elsewhere.
>
> Migration and conquest play an intermittent role in redistributing populations and changing their relations .... another set of processes effect changes of identity in individual and groups .... boundaries may persist despite what may figuratively be called the osmosis of groups through them.
>
> (ibid. p. 21)

Clearly the maintenance of a polyethnic system requires changes and often violent changes in those who man them.

Barth recognizes the possibility of injustice and inequality in a section dealing with ethnic groups and stratification. A group may control the means of production held by another group or may exercize control of assets which are valued by other groups in the system. In these cases, ethnicity overlaps with 'stratification'. But, according to Barth, while ethnicity may sometimes involve stratification, stratification does not always involve ethnicity. It may be impossible in that stratification may not deal with bounded strata at all but simply on the notion of scales 'and the recognition of an ego-centred level of 'people who are just like us' versus those more select and those more vulgar'.

Finally, Barth deals with a case in which ethnicity might be a stigma. Surprisingly, this is not the case in which one group categorizes another without its consent and discriminates against it, but the more restricted case of an incorporated group which can use its own culture for limited purposes only and is forced to live large parts of its life operating in terms of the culture of the incorporating group.

> In the total social system, all sectors of activity are organized by statuses open to members of the majority group, while the status system of the minority has relevance only to relations within the minority and only to some sectors of activity.
>
> (ibid. p. 31)

One culture here is thought of as having wider applicability and, therefore, superiority as compared with another. Members of the ethnic group with the inferior culture must, therefore, partially assimilate, keeping their own culture for limited purposes.

A Critique of Barth's Theory

One of the problems in dealing with Barth's theory is that the practical and theoretical problem with which one starts is really a problem only for ethnologists. It is because they had previously concentrated on studying the internal social structure of primitive peoples, often living on islands, but always conceivable in isolation, that those like Barth who were called upon to study more complex societies were forced to face what seemed a wholly new question, namely 'Who is a Pathan and who is not a Pathan?' or 'What and where is the boundary of Pathan-ness?' Even more, when anthropologists turned their attention to Western societies, they had to ask whether there were ethnic groups which could be isolated for study at all.

This was no problem for those not professionally in the habit of studying peoples in isolation. Their problem was to ask what bases

there were in the societies which they were studying for the formation of groups. Kinship is such a basis, so is territoriality and so
also perhaps is class interest and the associational structure which
arises in pursuit of such interest. Ethnicity does not automatically
come to mind as one of these bases except in societies to which
groups of outsiders have, for one reason or another, been added,
or unless the concept of ethnicity is used so loosely as to be
tautologically defined as cultural sameness.

Barth's interest lies not in his professional defence of the right
of an ethnologist to a subject matter, but in his attempt to argue
that despite the overlapping and co-residence of groups, ethnicity
remains a very important basis of identification and identity.
According to him

> A categorized description is an ethnic ascription when it classifies a
> person in terms of his most general identity defined by his origin and
> background.
>
> (ibid. p. 13)

In other words, ethnic identity remains in complex societies and is
extremely important. It classifies people according to 'origins and
background' and does so on a more general level than, say,
kinship.

One might dispute whether this is true in complex industrial
society. Leaving aside immigrants, do we really classify people in
terms of their most general origin and background? Origin and
background beyond the immediate fact of kinship most often refer
to class background and education. Hence Abner Cohen (1974)
gives as an example of 'ethnicity' the way upper class men in the
City of London sound each other out as to their schooling, culture
and tastes before getting down to business, but this refers to the
style of life of a status group, not an ethnic group. Ethnicity is
usually a quite minor theme if it is taken to mean descent from a
particular culture.

The next thing to notice about Barth's work is that he refers
without reservation to ethnic 'groups' rather than 'quasi-groups' as
we have done. This is because, in common with other anthropologists, he uses such terms loosely. It is important, therefore, to
consider what exactly he does mean by a group in this context.

In the first place, the term seems to be cognitively defined. A
group is defined in terms of recognizable and shared qualities of
individuals, so that an individual with these qualities counts as
inside, and without them, as outside. But this is what most people
would call a category. Much more important is the notion that the
individual who classifies others in terms of such qualities sees

himself or herself as having duties towards the other and as being entitled to expect certain behaviour from the other, as well as having feelings of enjoyment in the presence of the other. These may be described as communal responses. But the existence of even these attitudes does not constitute a group. They refer to potentialities for action only and the important thing about the ethnic collectivities which Barth is describing is that they may provide a basis for group formation, just as a class-in-itself provides a basis for the organization of a class-for-itself.

In referring to these collectivities as groups, Barth both overstates and understates their importance. He overstates it in that they are not capable of collective action as groups should be. He understates it in that he fails to note that when such groups are formed within and from the collectivity, they start with a degree of emotional and moral involvement which mere associations do not have. A class based purely on common interest has difficulty in forming organizations because the spur provided by emotional bonding is not there to start with. When ethnic groups are formed from an ethnic collectivity, however, they start out with strong ties of this kind. This is the sense in which ethnicity and the existence of the ethnic collectivity constitutes a valuable resource for collective action.

Barth also fails to make allowance for the degree of uncertainty in and conflict over ethnic exceptions. While he sees that one of the main features of his ethnic 'groups' is

> a membership which identifies itself, and is identified by others as constituting a category . . . .
>
> (ibid. p. 11)

he does not question whether self-identification might not clash with identification by others. But clearly a man or woman might claim to be 'still a Pathan' without having that claim recognized by others. More than this, the group he sees as an ethnic group might be seen by others as a class, estate or status group, as we saw at the beginning of Chapter 2. There is, therefore, much less stability in ethnic statuses and ethnic ascriptions than Barth envisages, and this is particularly important where ethnicity vies with other criteria of identification, as it does in modern industrial societies.

For all that we have said, however, it might still be argued that in the micro-sociology of modern societies, where we are interested in all the bases in terms of which individuals categorize each other, ethnicity in the sense in which Barth refers to it is an important principle. And this is particularly important when Barth refers to 'sets of prescriptions' 'allowing for articulation in some sectors or domains of activity' and 'sets of proscriptions' preventing ethnic interaction. At least, these are important questions when one considers the way in which members of clearly delineated ethnic groups confront each other (e.g. Indians, West Indians and Native British in British society).

What is more questionable is the extension of this sociology to the macro-level and the use to explain the relations which hold on the macro-level between ethnic quasi-groups. We have suggested that very often in complex polyethnic situations the relations between these quasi-groups are those of classes, estates and castes. As such they involve domination and subordination and, probably, conflict. This element of conflict is suppressed in Barth's account.

According to him, the nature of a plural society is to be found in the fact that there is a system such that there are sets of prescriptions and proscriptions in relations between one group and another. But is it ever adequate in sociology to offer an explanation which implicitly begins 'there is a system such that . . . .'? Surely the questions may be asked 'Where does this system come from?' or 'Who proposes this system?' Here it turns out that the system arises because it is imposed by the dominant power.

Furnivall, it is clear, did not regard the relations of the market place in his plural society as being mainly a set of prescriptions and proscriptions governing social etiquette. He regarded them as market relations and market relations of a peculiar sort, in which the common will that surrounded such relations in Western societies was not present, so that fraud and force, which were outlawed there, were in fact permitted in colonial circumstances. People were exploiting other people.

This means that another and much more complex type of explanation has to be given of the plural society. As exploited groups, the ethnic groups being exploited by the colonialists must be thought of as rejecting any but the minimal social intercourse with their exploiters. They work, that is to say, for money. Outside of this 'callous cash nexus', to use Marx's phrase, they interact with their own kind and look to their own kind for solidarity and support. On the other hand, the exploiters are only interested in using the labour of the ethnic groups. It is for them a commodity. It is in the nature of such a commodity that it does not lead to wider social ties.

No doubt Barth would argue that this is not inconsistent with his characterization of the intergroup relations of a plural society. We do admit that there are prescriptions (to enter the labour market and exchange work for wages) and proscriptions (not to allow this act to lead to any form of moral association or community), and that is all that he would ask. It does, however, seem important to recognize that the nature of the 'system' in a colonial labour market has long-term consequences. Quite clearly the ethnic groups in such a situation might revolt.

There are other surprising things in Barth's account which suggest the same blandness and complacency. The demographic adjustment necessary to sustain the system apparently involves conquest, forced migration and mortality, and there is the rather strange notion that without complementarity there can be no ethnic relations. It is hard to read these observations without concluding that for Barth the study of ethnic relations is confined to situations in which groups comply with the demands of these masters. Perhaps it is. But the dynamics of ethnic relation systems depend profoundly on the wider dynamics of the class system, which as Marx once said can be 'understood in its contradictions and revolutionized in practice', (1957).

Underlying this tendency towards accepting the status quo is a kind of functionalism which Barth shares with other anthropologists of functionalist and structural-functionalist persuasion. He seems to regard social situations as explained if he can show the system of ideas which underlies them. But such systems of ideas are constraints of a peculiar sort. According to our view outlined in Chapter 1, they refer not to 'things' but to the actions of others which can be called into question, opposed and altered. No doubt political realism would lead us to take seriously the degree of constraint which the system imposes, but there is no need to be fatalist about it. Systems can be changed and very often are changed by political action, including the action of ethnic minorities.

Wallman's theory of Urban Ethnicity

Barth's ideas have been applied and developed in Britain by Wallman, and her development of his theories is of especial interest because she applies them in contexts where race and colour differences between West Indians and Asians on the one hand and native English on the other are involved.

In her more recent essay (Mason and Rex 1986), Wallman goes out of her way to distinguish her work from that of the sorts of theorist discussed here. As she says:

> relative to the social scientists, anthropologists are seldom professionally concerned with vertical relations between ethnic groups and macro-state structures and they rarely undertake studies of offical policies (or lack of them) for minority groups, or of social stratification and minority status as such.
>
> (ibid)

One might, of course, point out that many anthropologists like M. G. Smith, or even Barth, have been concerned with precisely these areas. It is, however, useful to know that what Wallman intends is not concerned with this. While in no way accepting that anthropologists should not be concerned with macro-political issues, it will be interesting to consider what she has to say as an account of what is involved in more fine-grained studies of ethnic relations. This was of most interest in Barth and it is important to consider what is involved in such studies in Britain.

As Wallman sees it:

> under a common rubric of interest in lateral relations at the micro-level, anthropological studies can be distinguished according to whether they concentrate on relations in an 'ethnic community', or relations between one ethnic group and another; or on the possibility of some level of dynamic relation between inside and outside in a particular circumstance .... differences of this sort do not indicate that the various studies are built upon different theoretical premises.
>
> (ibid.)

Traditional anthropology addressed itself to the first of these tasks, Barth and Smith were more concerned with the second. Wallman deals with both the second and the third.

Wallman, even more than Barth, tends to argue in terms of metaphors and analogies, so that it is rather difficult to operationalize her theories and to envisage testing them. Thus she quotes with approval the famous statement of Barth that

> Ethnic categories are organizational vessels that may be given varying amounts and forms of content in different socio-cultural systems.
>
> (Barth 1969, p. 14)

but herself prefers the notion devised from Y. Cohen (1969) that boundaries may be thought of as like balloons. She goes on to modify the notion and to suggest that they are even more like tea-bags.

Before we turn to the explication of these metaphors, however, it is interesting to note that Wallman does not believe that it is important from the point of view of boundary theory to distinguish between race and ethnicity. As she puts it:

> Epistemologically the two terms are alike; in both cases it is the classifier's perception of choice or immutability which is decisive; the differences observed and the way they are interpreted say as much about the classifier as about the classified .... Once clear that

ethnic relations follow on the social construction of difference, phenotype falls into place as one element in the repertoire of ethnic boundary markers.

(ibid.)

Those who are interested in the study of 'racism' then may wish to distinguish between markers thought to be immutable and those which are subject to change, but clearly there is a common theory of boundaries in which colour and phenotype are on a par with differences of culture. The point is that they are available as potential markers but may or may not be used. The more important business is showing the circumstances in which they are used.

The metaphors of the balloon and the tea-bag have the following significances. The skin of the balloon is seen as being subject to two kinds of pressure, from inside and from outside, and its size and location vary acccordingly. So also the boundary of an ethnic group will alter when subject to pressure from the outside environment or from inside the group. The tea-bag notion on the other hand draws attention to the fact that individual members of the enclosed group might, like tea-leaves, find their way through the bag into the tea-pot. The important point here is that despite the escapes, the tea-bag and the ethnic boundary continue to exist.

Boundaries are also said to have two aspects. One is 'structural and organizational'. The boundary marks the interface of one system and another. The second is subjective. It marks the difference between 'us' and 'them'. It indicates 'identity':

A social boundary is about the organization of society, no more and no less than it is about the organization of experience.

(Wallman 1979, p. 207)

It may be looked at from the point of view of 'us' or 'them', and from its meaning in terms of interface and identity. Wallman seeks to express this in Figure 10.

Wallman believes that 'the boundary process more relevant to intergroup relations of the sort called 'racial-ethnic' is shown by linking the top left to bottom right.

The purpose of Wallman's own work and that which she proposes is to map the variations in the way in which boundaries are drawn. In what is actually an immensely complicated argument she invites us to consider whether ethnicity or some other factor is the basis of a boundary, if so by what markers it is recognized, in what way a boundary might move and in what situations it might move. The main thesis, however, is that of the situational determination of boundaries. We define a boundary in terms of markers which might suit our interests in a particular context. On other occasions

	Identity	*Interface*
Inside (us)	We identify 'us' in opposition to 'them'. We use the boundary for our purposes according to our needs/at this time/in this context.	The boundary around the familiar, the normal, the unproblematic.
Outside (them)	'They' identify themselves by contrast to the rest of us. They use the boundary for their purposes.	The beginning of another system. Performance, appearance, activity, social or symbolic structure is different.

Figure 10. Wallman's theory of aspects of boundaries

(ibid. p. 207)

and in different contexts we might use different markers and place the boundary elsewhere, and we might well find that although we put the boundary with 'them' at one point, 'they' might see it as being elsewhere and as being defined by different markers.

The processes here are infinitely various and it is, therefore, helpful that Wallman provides us with some examples of boundary marking in operation.

The first example is a racially mixed residential population whose homes have been placed in a 'housing action area' by a local authority and who have to define their position both in relation to each other and in relation to the local bureaucracy. In this case, ethnicity is not important as a boundary marker. Black and White residents unite as 'us' against the bureaucrats as 'them'.

The second example is South Asians in South London. These include Indians, Pakistanis, Bangladeshis and Kashmiris, Hindus, Sikhs and Muslims, and Punjabi, Gujerati and Urdu speakers. Outside the British context and even within it, these separate groups draw 'us' and 'them' boundaries between each other. But in the British context, they find that they are all treated as Asians and begin to have common interests as Asians. Other Asians become 'we' and the British 'them'.

The third example is British reactions to the presence in their midst of *British-born* Blacks. Since traditional boundaries in imperial and colonial terms were between British who were rich and powerful and Colonial Blacks who were poor and powerless, the emergence of British Blacks created cognitive dissonance. Whites became ambivalent in their attitudes to Blacks, though they might resolve this by deciding that successful Blacks were not really Black, and the Blacks are able to manipulate the situation (Wallman 1979). Elsewhere Wallman suggests that Whites might use this boundary to preserve their own sense of identity (Mason and Rex 1986).

In her later essay, Wallman draws wider conclusions from her study of interethnic action in a housing action area. She finds that, not only in the narrow housing action area but in the wider locality, this particular group emphasizes local residence as the basis of we-group formation. On the other hand, there is a not-too-distant inner city area where ethnicity is the basis of group formation. The choice of locality rather than ethnicity as the basis for communal action is, she believes, due to the degree of openness of networks in the first area.

It is difficult to draw any overall conclusion about racial and ethnic relations from all this, even though it is useful to note that, looked at in the fine grain, boundaries between we-groups and they-groups are infinitely flexible. Ethnicity may or may not be involved as a boundary marker, the actual markers chosen will vary according to the circumstances, and the location of the boundary might alter.

Against this picture of infinite flexibility and the opportunistic use of boundaries, some anthropologists would hold that it is important to recognize that even when ethnicity is not used as a marker, it is always there, as Wallman puts it, 'cool in the belly'. Wallman believes that it is important when such potential boundary markers are 'heated up'. She says that this often occurs when the actors develop identity investments because of their economic or political interests. Sometimes, however, identity has no significance in terms of interest. It might be 'pure affect'. For whatever reason, the need for identity will lead to the adoption of strong boundary markers, including those based on ethnicity.

Undoubtedly, Wallman draws our attention to many complex themes in the study of boundary processes and we may agree with her that

If we can establish how many criteria of difference are imposed on a single boundary—at the level of meaning, at the level of action, in

what context by whom and for what purposes, we may begin to
monitor even the most complex of boundary processes, and to
understand mechanisms of social and 'racial' differentiation to
better effect.

(Wallman 1979, p. 215)

A Critique of Wallman's Theory

The business of mapping so complex an area involves choices of
emphasis and it would seem that Wallman's own emphasis is upon
the fact that boundary processes are not dependent upon macro-
political processes and that ethnicity as well as race may not be as
important as other bases for dividing the world into 'us' and
'them'. What would be more interesting to try to connect studies
of this kind with the study of 'macro-state structures' and 'social
stratification and minority status as such'.

If one looks at Wallman's examples, they all have strong links
with the political system at one level or another. Her account of the
interethnic movement in the housing action area is strongly
reminiscent of my own theory of housing classes. The case of the
British 'Asians' is indicative of racist thinking by the British, and
the problem of the Black British is again a problem which only
arises because of earlier generalizations made about Blacks.

My own view is, to use Wallman's phrase, that both class and
ethnicity are 'there' 'cool in the belly', and that they will be exploited as and when the political situation heats up. Class-in-itself
can become class-for-itself. Of course, the transition to groups-for-
themselves does not occur easily or automatically and it *is* important that we should look at all the processes which are involved
before situations heat up. But it is not necessary to exclude from
consideration the possibility of a situation in which either ethnicity
or class or both together operate as the main means of boundary
marking because people have become conscious of their interests,
have seen those interests in conflict with the thems of the other class
and ethnic group, and have organized to pursue shared interests
against the other side.

The argument might well be put on Wallman's behalf that the
empirical evidence is against such an account. But is it? Is it not
precisely because limited indices of boundary behaviour have been
used that so apolitical a picture emerges? Do these residents not
read newspapers, do they not vote, do they not engage in trades
union activity? A wider and more balanced assembly of the
evidence would show that other forms of consciousness emerged

from these sources. If the over-politicized view of class and race/ethnic struggle which is common in the political sociology of race relations needs correcting through a look at the fine grain, so the underpoliticized view also needs correcting by a further and systematic look at the economic and political relations in which all men and women in a modern industrial society are necessarily involved.

Conclusion

Earlier in this chapter we suggested that the anthropologists' approach to ethnicity might perhaps be complementary to that used here in that it dealt only with cases of 'benign' ethnicity. From our account of the theories of Barth and Wallman, it can be seen that this is not the case. They do attempt to deal with processes of conflict. Indeed the whole notion of the flexibility of boundaries is based upon disagreement. Nevertheless, boundary theory as a whole suggests explanations in terms of the existence of systems of thought which are taken as decisive in the determination of social structure. In contrast, the approach taken here is one in which structure and system are seen as the result of conflicting pressures.

It would be easier to locate the anthropologists' position if one found that they were dealing with interethnic interaction as such divorced from any question of interests. Again and again, though, Barth and Wallman suggest that it is precisely in situations of conflict of interest that ethnicity ceases to be simply 'cool in the belly' but becomes heated up and active. The main exception to this, according to Wallman, is the case in which ethnicity is used as a means of achieving identity.

It may be, however, that the great interest of the anthropologists' theories is precisely their concern with the cognitive mapping which individuals do prior to action. Ethnicity and class both appear in this mapping as potential bases for collective action. They are there 'cool in the belly' or 'in themselves'. Why men come to act and how they come to act, that is to say, how these potentialities are converted into actuality, is another question. Just possibly we might admit that the perception of difference itself is a cause of action with or against the category of people perceived to be different. But that is surely a small part of the whole business of sociology or social anthropology. The interesting point about Barth and Wallman is that they don't confine their studies in this way. In so doing they are forced to move from studying the benign to studying the malign and political aspects of race and ethnic relations. The only remaining point of difference in approach then is that they concentrate on the fine-grained micro-aspects of social interaction. These, our argument suggests, have to be seen within a larger and much more conflictual perspective.

Chapter 6

Racism, Institutionalized and Otherwise

Action, Language and Race

The emphasis in the previous chapter has been on social structure. The third part of the definition of a race relations situation given in Chapter 3, however, emphasizes the important of the ideological justification of such structures. It was said there that a differentiating feature of race relations situations was that they were justified by powerful groups 'in terms of some sort of deterministic theory (usually a biological or genetic one) which suggested that the position of the different categories could not be other than it was'. We now have to consider whether argument about such theoretical or ideological justification can be thought of as having a curative role and whether the injustices inherent in racial conflict, discrimination, exploitation and oppression can be put right or overcome by an exposure and rejection of theories.

The Marxian answer to this question, which would also be given by many non-Marxist sociologists, is that 'it is not the consciousness of men that determines their existence, but their social existence that determines their consciousness' (Marx 1962). Before we can accept this, however, we must consider more closely what is meant by 'social existence'. More complex answers to this question are suggested by the work of Pareto and by the American phenomenologists, Berger and Luckmann.

Pareto (1935) assumes that much of our social action is of a non-logical kind. We do not first set out our goals and then choose the scientifically appropriate means for attaining them as we would do in logical action thus:

Setting   of   goal—Development   of   theory—Choice   of Appropriate Means—Action

Rather we begin with certain sentiments requiring expression, and at the same time as we act we offer a verbal account of that act, called a residue. The model of such action is

The residue is never a rational or logical theory, although we often seek subsequently to rationalize it in terms of another verbal utterance, which Pareto calls a 'derivation'. In fact, as we study actions we often have to start with these 'derivations'. It is when we analyze these into their variable and constant parts that we discover the residues. There is almost no limit to the variety of the rationalizations or derivations we may offer, but underlying them are certain repeated non-logical theories. Economics is the theory of logical action but sociology deals with these non-logical theories or alternative logics.

The implication of Pareto's theory for the study of race relations is that instead of assuming that consciousness determines action, we should assume that individuals engage in interaction with other individuals or quasi-groups for reasons to do with conflict, exploitation and oppression, and in the course of so doing give an account of their action. Our task is to see through the rationalizations and to discover the constants which determine such action. There is no need to follow Pareto in his account of the constant part of theories, the residues. He speaks of the residues of combination, of the persistence of aggregates, of the manifestation of sentiments through external acts, residues of sociability, residues of the integrity of the individual and sexual residues. Those relating to the persistence of aggregates and the integrity of the individual would probably be most relevant to race and ethnic relations. It would probably be better, however, if we were merely to posit basic processes of human need fulfilment which underly the actions rationalized by derivations.

Pareto's approach appears to downgrade the importance of theory compared with those who see all behaviour as determined by theory. But he also upgrades it by pointing out that verbalizations and theorization go along with behaviour. There is no pure social existence without theorization of some sort. Human action may therefore be observed and classified on two levels. One deals with actual behaviour, the other with the verbal justification of that behaviour. Racialist behaviour like any other goes along with racist theory.

Pareto's conception of the unity of theory and practice, however, is somewhat distorted and peculiar in that it is especially concerned to differentiate economic and non-economic behaviour. Of greater relevance to our argument is the work of the phenomenological and symbolic interactionist schools who have recognized that social existence involves, as Weber put it, one actor orienting his conduct to another, and that this in turn is only possible if these two actors share the same intersubjective world.

We create such an intersubjective world by agreeing to attach labels to our experience. In so doing we make the claim that they are in some sense the same experiences which other people have had, and we also connect them with other experiences of our own, in that meanings do not stand by themselves but have definite relations to each other. If I say that I am seeing a chair, I am saying that I am having an experience which is similar to some of your experiences, but also different and related to other experiences of yours and mine which I describe as seeing a table. In using language about the physical world, therefore, we must already hold implicit shared theories about the world and how it works.

In ordinary speech, however, this is far from being simply a cognitive business. At this level no distinction is made between saying something exists and giving advice or instruction on how it is to be treated, or saying whether it is good or beautiful or sacred. Thus a Christian who learns to use the word 'cross' or 'communion' does not simply learn to attach a particular label to a particular thing. He acquires a knowledge of the appropriate attitudes to these symbols and in so doing acquires not simply a scientific but a moral and religious education.

In our own Western culture, of course, we have sought to distinguish the question 'What is this object?' from all questions about aesthetic or moral qualities. There is a set of procedures we call 'science' by which we arrive at a picture of the world that is more relevant for a number of purposes, especially for the purposes of controlling that world. But this is not the only possible or even the most relevant picture. We do not make chemical analyses of the substances used in a religious sacrament in order to understand the sacraments better. Nor are we helped in appreciating a picture by a geometrical analysis of its form. There is more to life than science can tell us.

If, however, it is true that our langugae is loaded with aesthetic and moral meanings so far as objects in the physical world are concerned, how much more true must it be in the case of social objects. Here we rarely distinguish between the question 'What is this?' and 'How should I feel and act towards this?' The goal of Positivism has been to eliminate this confusion both for scientific purposes and in everyday life (Lundberg 1939, Chase 1938), but it is not a goal which has been or is likely to be realized.

In any case, it is not clear what a scientific way of looking at and labelling social objects would be like. We might seek to replace the observation 'this is a Jew' or 'this is a Negro' with a statement that 'this is a human being' in order to eliminate the moral and political overtones of the terms 'Jew' and 'Negro', but we would nonetheless be making implicit reference to some other moral and political code which asserts that the universal qualities of men are more important than their differences. Not surprisingly, therefore, there is no known society in which social actors are not categorized in terms much narrower than 'human being' and these categorizations imply a set of moral duties and a form of social organization.

The simplest form of categorization of social objects is seen in systems of kinship terminology. Such a terminology constitutes a primitive society's own sociology. Unlike a system of personal names, the system of kinship terms brings into being a group structure. It makes clear what rights and duties any individual has not merely vis-a-vis ego but in relation to every other individual.

There will, however, be individuals to whom ego cannot relate in terms of kinship terminology. Some of these will be grouped in classificatory groups such as clans. The position of an individual in one group vis-à-vis an individual in another group will follow from the relationship which any individual in the one group is held to have with an individual in the other. A social system based upon a normative consensus may be built up in this way, often involving totemic classes. What differentiates such a system from the sort of system we have discussed in previous chapters dealing with composite societies is that the system of rights and duties which it implies is a means of achieving a division of labour, through which overall group ends can be attained. There is no question of the group which is singled out in this way becoming the target of hostile policies. This may be the case with people who fall right outside of the tribe or its constituent classes, in which case there may be parallels with race relations problems depending on whether the groups are in conflict with one another over resources. But the outside in such a system may be simply an individual for whom it is impossible to define rights and duties rather than an outright enemy.

In many cases which Barth considers in his account of ethnic boundaries, even the relations of these larger groups may be complementary. They may occupy separate ecological niches, they may have separate political territories or they may perform complementary economic roles. But where such complementarity does not exist, groups of outsiders or enemies may be defined, and very often they will be defined, not simply for cognitive purposes, but in such a way as to mobilize specific attitudes toward them. Thus a Spanish historian refers to American Indians as 'lazy and vicious, melancholic, cowardly and in general a lying and shiftless people' (Hanke 1959). Similarly Van Riebeck, the first Governor of the Cape Colony, refers to the Hottentots as 'stupid, dull stinking people' (de Kiewiet 1948).

Such statements, which are the normal stuff of intergroup relations in colonial circumstances, are clearly not simply intellectual responses. Instead of saying 'this type of person is my competitor for resources and in attempting to realize my goals I have to stop him attaining his', the individual makes the much simpler response 'these people are evil'. Such statements have the characteristics of Pareto's residues. They are not deductions from some higher theory. Along with acts which they accompany, they are themselves forms of agression. Once this is understood, the problem of 'curing racism' becomes not one of correcting theory on the abstract level, but of dealing with these basic acts of aggression. Of course one will find that reasons of all kinds are adduced in support of these basic verbal acts of aggression—theological, biological, historical and cultural—but the use of these reasons as justification is precisely what Pareto meant when he referred to derivations based on verbal proofs. Faced with this sort of data, the real problem is to look for the 'constant part' or 'residue' which underlies the 'derivation'. Here the residue is simply a verbal act of aggression rather than any of the subtle alternative logics to which Pareto refers.

The Problematic of Racism

It is important to understand that in recent years the most common approach of sociologists and politicians to resisting racism and racialism has not been based on the kind of analysis above. Nor has the whole sociology of race relations. Rather, sociologists have seen themselves as having the task of finding tendencies to racism largely on the level of theory and proposing ways in which it might be cured, with little serious discussion taking place about the relationship between theories and social structure. This is evident in the way in which the problem of race relations was discussed in relation in Nazi Germany, in relation to South Africa, in the United States and, more recently, in Britain.

In the case of Nazi Germany, the central problem is the extermination of seven million Jews. The usual explanation is that it was the consequence of racism on the part of the Nazi leaders and party members. They were thought to have falsely claimed that the Jews were a race and that their racial characteristics included tendencies towards various sorts of political behaviour, ranging from capitalist exploitation to Communist subversion. In its most developed form, Nazi doctrine was based upon a false theory of physical anthropology which suggested that 'Aryans' were a superior race. The way to prevent the recurrence of genocide in the future, therefore, was seen as lying in the correction of these false beliefs, both at the highest level of biological theory and at the level of popular beliefs. What is not usually discussed is the nature of the social structure of Germany and the place of the Jews within it. This is by no means to suggest that the theory followed from the structure because it gave a correct account of it. It does suggest, however, that it is worth considering whether there were strains in the German social structure which made the occurrence of scapegoating likely, and whether the social and economic position of the Jews as well as their distinctive appearance made them suitable candidates for scapegoating as a group. An enquiry along these lines would start with an analysis of structure and, on the empirical level, would study the behaviour of individuals pursuing hostile courses of action against the Jews. The Republic of South Africa occupies a similar place in the international political conscience of the world today to that occupied by Nazi Germany in the 1930s. The South African Nationalists are seen as believing in racist theories, often backed by fundamentalist religion, about the inferiority of the Black races. This is seen as being of the essence of what is called the doctrine of 'apartheid'. In this case, there is a greater understanding amongst sociologists of the structural basis of race relations, but the popular view which still informs many sociological investigations is that the structure of South African society follows from the racist theory of apartheid.

Thinking in the United States was influenced after the 1939-45 War by refugee scholars who explained the phenomenon of racism in terms of personality variables like authoritarianism. At that time

very little was said about the relevance of the theory of race relations for Blacks. Myrdal, called on as an outsider to investigate the
so-called Negro problem, however, saw it as representing a dilemma
on the part of White America, which was committed by its constitution to principles of equality, but which in practice tolerated
segregation and racial domination. In the wake of political changes
in the 1950s and Black resistence in the 1960s, America became
much more committed to rooting out 'racism'. It was then
discovered, however, that very often discrimination and disadvantage amongst Blacks was not the result of intentional policies or of
psychological racism amongst those who discriminated. This led to
the adoption of the problematic concept of 'institutional racism',
which will be discussed below.

Finally, Britain began to face race relations problems with the
settlement of about one million immigrants from the Indian sub-
continent, from the Caribbean and from East Africa. The adoption
of racially selective immigration controls after the arrival of the
bulk of the male workers in this population then produced a crisis
of conscience. The government was assailed by its critics for having
made concessions to 'racism' by adopting a 'racist' immigration
policy, and the government itself drew attention to the dangers of
racism in the support for the more extreme policies of Enoch
Powell, the Conservative Member of Parliament, and of neo-Nazi
groups like the National Front. Eventually the policy of anti-racism
became widespread and attempts were made to develop educational
policies which would eliminate even unconscious racism amongst
gatekeepers in the social services and in society at large.

Given the approach of this book, racism was to be expected in
all of the cases mentioned. The Jews were the chosen scapegoat of
a Nazi Government facing economic and political crises. 'Racism'
in South Africa was the inevitable accompaniment of a situation in
which White employers exploited Black labour. In the United
States there was not only the historical legacy of a slave-plantation
society, but Black migrants from that society were seeking to compete for employment and housing with White Americans and White
immigrants in the North. Finally, in Britain, there was a legacy of
a colonial society in which the colonized people were regarded as
inferior, and an industrial and social structure in which socially
mobile Whites had abandoned jobs and other social positions and
Black workers were brought in to fill these positions. The problems
were not those which arose from racism either on the psychological
or the theoretical level, but questions of social structure and inequality. Curing racism would require either that the inequalities in
these societies should be eliminated or else that policies should be

developed to ensure that racial and ethnic difference were not used
as a basis for assigning men and women to unequal positions.

Psychological Explanations of 'Racism'

Undoubtedly, the more influential theory in the study of race relations in the 1950s was that which sought to explain racist behaviour
as due to tensions within the personality system. This was originally
developed by a team of psychologists. Although most of them were
of empiricist and positivist background, they became associated
with a leading member of the Frankfurt School of Critical Theory,
T.W. Adorno (Adorno *et al.* 1950).

The Frankfurt School had been forced to modify its own version
of Marxist theory because it had seemed too rationalistic. German
workers simply did not behave as they might have been expected to
do in the light of rationalistic theories of behaviour. To explain the
discrepancies, the School had recruited the psychoanalyst Erich
Fromm, who was eventually to give his own account of
psychologically disturbed behaviour in his *Escape From Freedom*
(see M. Jay 1973, E. Fromm 1942). According to this account, it
was characteristic of the modern age that it presented human beings
with a possibility of freedom of which they were terrified because
they had been inadequately socialized. The individual fleeing from
being alone with himself sought escape through sick personal relations of a sadistic or masochistic kind, through retreating into
work, or through dependence upon a political or religious leader.

The last of these notions was independently investigated by
Adorno and his colleagues. They suggested that there was a type of
personality that scored highly on the so-called 'F-scale', which
measured willingness to submit to a form of rigid authority,
coupled with aggression against those who reject this authority.
Such individuals look at the world in a tough-minded way, have a
paranoid fear of outsiders and tend to think in dichotomous terms.
People who scored highly on this scale were likely to be anti-semitic
and to show prejudice towards Blacks and outgroups of all kinds.
They were also likely to be individuals who had had a strict family
unbringing or adhered to fundamentalist religious beliefs.

Although this theory exercized great influence in America, it was
subject to a number of difficulties. One was that both left and right
wing authoritarians, although they held rigid beliefs, were not
necessarily prejudiced against minorities.

The central difficulty about the Authoritarian Personality
School, however, was that the number of people in most populations

who had high scores on the F-scale was usually small and 'racism' was often a form of majority behaviour. It explained why people who became Nazis were racist and even why racialist policies were adopted when a minority of Nazis exercized power. What it could not explain was the racist thinking and the racialist practice of majorities amongst ruling groups. This certainly seemed to be the problem in countries like South Africa.

Another and simpler version of Freudian theory was developed by John Dollard and his colleagues. According to this theory, serious frustration leads quite naturally to aggressive behaviour against the frustrator. If, however, the frustrator is in a position where he cannot be attacked, the aggression will be stored up and eventually directed against a more suitable target (i.e. someone or some group which is unable to protect itself against aggression, Dollard *et al.* 1939). Dollard used this explanation to explain White behaviour in the Deep South (Dollard 1957).

There may well be some value in this type of explanation in that it would explain why an individual should act aggressively against competitors. It is not easy to see, however, why we should apply it more to a ruling group like the Whites of the Deep South rather than to those whom they ruled and oppressed and frustrated. In fact, the theory of frustration and aggression would serve best to explain the aggression of oppressed groups rising in revolt.

Racism and the Sociology of Knowledge

Talcott Parsons has suggested that the sciences of social action involve reference to three systems, the social system, the personality system and the cultural system (Parsons, Shils *et al.* 1962). The explanation of racist thinking and racialist behaviour which we have just been discussing involves the second of these. Another possibility, however, is that what happens on the social level is at least in part determined by what happens on the cultural level. Individuals might be perfectly sane and undisturbed on the personality level and yet be forced to act through a particular language or culture which they have inherited. This is a matter we have discussed earlier in this chapter. The very words we use to label social objects have meanings which are related to other meanings and which have an effective as well as a cognitive content. We may through a process of education displace this cultural inheritance by putting another in its place. We might, for example, eliminate the use of the term 'Jew' or 'Black' in its current meaning and see that its implications have to do with universally shared rights of man.

What we cannot do is to eliminate culture and meaning systems altogether.

There is no reason why we should not admit that part of the total source of racist belief and racialist practice is to be found in the personality and the culture systems. This can be dealt with by those opposing racism, by curing or isolating those with disturbed personalities and by modifying culturally transmitted belief systems in a universalist direction. There does remain, however, the possibility that the problems arise within the *social* system itself and that they are only supported by tendencies on the personality and cultural system levels. It is to this we must now turn, emphasizing especially the problem of what has come to be called, following political and ideological events in the United States, 'institutional racism'.

The Problem of Institutional Racism

It should not come as a surprise that the social system has its own dynamic independent of the personality and cultural system. It was the study of this system that Talcott Parsons chose to make his own specialism (Parsons 1937 and 1950). True, much of his attention was devoted to normative controls which relate to the culture system, but these controls were concerned with ordering a process of interaction which turned as much as anything on the power relations of the parties. It is still the case that the study of the social system as such involves above all the power relations which exist between individuals, groups and quasi-groups and categories. When we say that an explanation is structural rather than psychological or cultural, we refer to pure social relations of this kind.

Before we turn to the specific theoretical development known as the problem of institutional racism, which is deeply concerned with social interaction as such, we must clear up a terminological confusion. This concerns the use of the terms racism and racialism. Conscious that there was a certain amount of confusion between the malign affects of bodies of ideas on the one hand and actual actions or practices on the other, a number of British sociologists (Banton 1969) suggested that we should use the term racism to refer to theories only and racialism to refer to the putting of those ideas into practice. Others suggested that we should use the term racialism to refer to practice without any suggestions that such practices were necessarily related to theory at all.

There were difficulties about getting this terminology adopted, however. Popular usage of the term racism was indiscriminate, and this usage increased as conflict in Britain and the United States deepened; many sociologists stuck to or adopted the use of the single term 'racism'; and several other languages, including especially French, had only one term.

Sociology, however, has ideological and political competitors whose speeches and writings are so influential that it is difficult for sociologists to ignore them and to insist upon pure academic discourse. If their work is to have any influence on public debate, they are bound to take up the terminology of the ideologies and politicians, even if in so doing they seek to use it with greater precision. This was certainly the case when American sociologists in the late sixties and early seventies had to respond to the use of the term 'institutional racism' as it was used by the Black American student teacher, Stokeley Carmichael (Carmichael and Hamilton 1968).

One can easily see why the term came to be used at a particular historical conjuncture. In 1954, the Brown versus the Board of Education decision had brought to fruition a process of attempting to use law to rectify the condition of Black Americans. Subsequently, Civil Rights Programmes had been instituted to outlaw discrimination in a wide variety of spheres, and Poverty Programmes to ensure that White and Black poor alike achieved a minimum of welfare. But now it seemed that even though racism was under attack and racial discrimination of an overt sort was being outlawed, Black people were still finding themselves at the bottom of the heap. Thus it was argued that even if government was not in the hands of racists and deliberate racial discrimination was outlawed, the very institutions which were normal to the functioning of American society were producing consequences which were disadvantageous to Blacks and represented a kind of 'institutional racism'.

Even though it is easy to understand how such a concept evolved, it is still possible to recognize that it was full of ambiguity. There would seem to be at least four meanings which could be attributed to it as follows:

(1) Although institutions are not governed by 'psychological' racists or by believers in racist theory, they may be subject to unconscious racism.

(2) Discrimination on racial grounds exists but is difficult to prove. The most important proof of its existence, however, is in the outcome in terms of Black or Minority disadvantage.

(3) The reasons why Blacks do badly out of ordinary market processes are hard to understand and their outcome difficult to rectify except by intervening in market processes to ensure that some Blacks do well.

(4) Discrimination on racial grounds does not exist, but the important fact is that the disadvantaged poor suffer and that a high proportion of the Black population are to be found amongst the disadvantaged poor.

We now need to look at each of these different interpretations in turn.

(1) Unconscious Racism

Very relevant to this question is the distinction we have drawn between 'psychological' racism and racism which is inherent in the belief system of a society. The first of these, however, is not what those who speak of institutionalized racism are referring to. It is in a very literal sense unconscious behaviour having to do with the defence mechanisms of the personality system. But this overt behaviour which is to be found in 'psychological' racists is recognized as racist and is precisely the sort of behaviour which the theorists of 'institutional racism' mean to exclude as unimportant.

Much more important is the racism inherent in the belief system of a society. Here actions are taken on the basis of common-sense reasoning, using common-sense knowledge of the world. Even in a society committed to universalism and equality of opportunity, such common-sense knowledge is marked by the use of stereotypes of minority individuals which are derogatory to them or which place them in questionable settings. This is inevitably the case with common-sense knowledge in a society with a history of war and imperialist involvement. Even liberal culture in such a society is impregnated with what are in effect racist and paternalist assumptions, as Wellman (1977) in the United States and Dummett (1973) in Great Britain have shown.

Central to plans for combating institutional racism is the proposal to re-educate social gatekeepers and the public at large through courses in 'ethnic or racial awareness' following lines suggested by Katz in the United States (1978). Such courses, if they are successful, must do nothing less than question the received assumptions of common-sense language and, indeed, must propose a wholly new social language. The task is on a par with ridding our language of 'sexist' assumptions.

More than this, however, it is necessary to institutionalize the new language. It must be shown that it is not an artificial language but one which authoritative figures in our society wish to see spoken. The relative success of such training in the United States has to do with this. There, as a result of Civil Rights Programmes, the United States Government from the President downwards had become publicly committed (as when President Johnson used the words of the Civil Rights song '*We* shall overcome') to ensuring equality for Blacks in American society. In these circumstances it made sense to tell, say, policemen or schoolteachers that they were required to learn and think in a new language. Acceptance of this new language was reinforced, moreover, by professional rewards in terms of posts and increments. It is much more difficult to imagine such training programmes being successful when they do not have central government backing as well as the backing of the press. Thus in Britian in the early 1980s, professional race relations workers were attempting to mount such courses but were seen as politicizing the professions in an undesirable way because what they were trying to do ran counter to the dominant political culture fostered by politicians and the national media.

It is perhaps too early to say how far programmes of this kind are likely to be successful. Their mere existence is indicative of the existence of anti-racist forces in a society, and shows that we need not accept that we are totally entrapped in the language we inherit. But it clearly does require a very strong commitment of a society to universalism if normal language and thinking are to be changed.

(2) Disadvantage and Discrimination

The term 'disadvantage' came into general use in the United States and Britain in the 1960s. It was used, however, in two quite different ways. According to the first, acts of discrimination by specific individuals existed, but it was difficult to prove except that in the outcome certain groups were shown to be systematically disadvantaged. According to the second, it was unknown whether or not discrimination was occurring, but in any case it did not matter, because other things could be done to correct the disadvantage which was evident in the outcome. We are concerned with the first usage in this section.

I find it useful to illustrate what is involved here by an example. In Britain in the 1960s there was a debate about the allocation of publicly built and owned houses for rent. Only rarely were there specific rules saying that Black people should not be offered these tenancies. In the event, however, one found that Black people were seriously underrepresented amongst those who obtained such houses. Their disadvantage was a clear indication that some kind of concealed discrimination was going on. Therefore the conclusion to be drawn was not simply that disadvantage was a fact and that the position of Blacks could be improved by dealing with disadvantage as such, but the renewed efforts had to be made to disclose the kinds of discrimination which were occurring.

Very important in this regard was the fact of indirect discrimination. In the example given, there were no rules against giving houses to Blacks but there were rules against considering applications from those who had recently arrived in the local authority area. There were also rules about overcrowding, which prevented the allocation of houses to large families. The first of these sets of rules especially, but the second to some extent, had the *effect* of preventing the allocation of houses to Black families. The problem then was one of indirect discrimination. Quite essential to fighting institutional racism then was the task of combating such indirect discrimination. This was different in that it always seemed possible to offer as a defence against the charge of indirect discrimination a claim that a rule was necessary on other non-racial grounds.

In the British case, laws were passed which dealt with this problem. According to the 1976 Race Relations Act, 'A person discriminates against another' if

> he applies to that other a requirement or condition which he applies equally to persons not of the same racial group as that other, but (1) which is such that the proportion of persons of the same racial group as that other who can comply with it is considerably smaller than the proportion of persons not of that racial group who can comply with it and (2) which he cannot show to be justifiable irrespective of the colour, race, nationality or ethnic or racial origin of the person to whom it is applied and (3) which is to the detriment of that other because he cannot comply with it.

(HMSO 1976)

The enforcement of such a law, however, still required its implementation by courts and tribunals and this was likely to be a difficult process.

(3) Disadvantage and Positive Discrimination

The alternative view of disadvantage is that it is not necessarily caused by discrimination at all or, if it is, such discrimination can be corrected at a later stage.

The normal processes of allocation in a complex society are through market or through formal bureaucratic systems operating according to the rules of formal justice. Under such systems Black people may be shown to do less well than Whites. They may get inferior jobs and inferior houses and do less well in the selective processes within the education system. In these circumstances, what is proposed is not any interference with the market or with allocation processes or with exams, but simply a wholesale bending of the rules so that a definite percentage outcome is achieved for Blacks.

It is surprising that the highest development of this policy should have been in the United States where the market and the system of formal justice might be thought of as having a near sacred quality. It is, therefore, a sign of how seriously the fight against institutional discrimination was taken that what amounted to a wholly new principle of social organization was adopted.

It was not intended, however, that such a system of predetermined outcomes should become a permanent feature of the society. The logic behind it may be called a 'logic of role models'. According to Gunnar Myrdal (1944), progress or otherwise in race relations matters followed a cumulative principle. If discrimination led to the appearance of poor, dirty, incapable people, there would be more discrimination because the people involved were poor, dirty and incapable. *Per contra*, if some individuals in the minority group were shown to be rich, clean and successful, discrimination would become more difficult and others in the minority group would emulate the rich, clean and successful. Eventually the whole process would therefore be self-sustaining. It was only necessary in the first place to establish the positions of the few by what came to be called positive discrimination or affirmative action.

Such positive discrimination and affirmative action could take a variety of forms. It might simply monitor the percentages of a minority who attained particular positions and consider what training might be necessary for a percentage, equal to that of the minority in the population at large, to be attained. But it might at the other extreme simply promote the incompetent in order to increase numbers of the minority in positions of authority and prestige. It is because the latter policy has been adopted, or because it has been thought to have been adopted, that there has been a backlash in the dominant group against such policies. The argument of those involved in the backlash is that 'these people have been given equal rights and have still not been successful; so they are now asking for more than their share.'

(4) Disadvantage and the Denial of Discrimination

One possible interpretation of Stokely Carmichael's argument was not that discrimination had to be fought, in that there needed to be positive discrimination on behalf of those in the minority who suffered disadvantage, but that there was no problem other than that of disadvantage as such. It was an particularly popular argument with radicals and socialists for whom the primary problem was one of class rather than race or ethnicity. The condition of the Blacks was simply a dramatic proof of the tendency of the capitalist society to produce inequality.

Such an argument was also popular in England when for a long time the civil servants responsible for the various social service ministries had been influenced by Fabianism. It was their habit to intervene on behalf of the poor and the disadvantaged amongst the native working class, and the condition of the Blacks was one with which they thought themselves familiar.

Throughout the 1960s and the 1970s the problem of racial disadvantage was seen as part of the general problem of disadvantage. The National Committee for Commonwealth Immigrants responded to allegations of discrimination in the housing field with a pamphlet entitled 'Areas of Special Housing Need' (1967). In policies developed for disadvantaged schools, immigrant needs were not particularly singled out. Indeed, the *presence* of immigrants was one of the *criteria* selected for declaring that a particular school was disadvantaged. The Urban Programme was set up to offer aid to the urban disadvantaged as such, and the Community Development Programmes which followed were concerned with the needs of all inner-city residents. The Department of Health and Social Security sponsored studies of cumulative disadvantage as such rather than the particular cumulative disadvantage of Black minorities. The Department of Education, asked to set up a centre for the study of minority problems in education, decided instead to create a Centre for the Study of Educational Disadvantage (Rex and Tomlinson 1979). Finally, the White Paper Policy for the Inner Cities (HMSO 1977), although it was widely thought of as being a policy for dealing with minorities, actually went out of its way to insist that it was not concerned with racial discrimination, but solely with the problem of the disadvantaged poor in the Inner City, arguing that any help given to this group must benefit the minorities. During this time it should also be said that other measures were adopted which were specifically directed at combating racial discrimination, but they were on the whole weakly applied until the urban disturbances of 1981, after which it was widely acknowledged that the disadvantage experienced by minorities required separate measures from those concerned with erasing disadvantage as such.

Curing a Society's 'racism'

Summarizing the experience referred to in the previous section, we may say that the attempt to eliminate institutional racism has led to confused policies which have as yet failed to achieve their objectives. We end this chapter then by considering some of the ways in which a society might deal with racialist practice and racism, institutionalized and otherwise, if it really decides to do so.

The qualification 'if it really decides to do so' is important, because it would seem unlikely that any complex modern society would eliminate all the practices and ideas which are grouped together under the headings 'racism' and 'racialism'. All thinking about social objects in such a society requires the use of what Schutz called typifications (1967), and when there is group conflict such typifications very easily become derogatory stereotypes. Why, then, if racial along with other forms of stereotyping is normal in any functioning society, should it be the case that a member of any society should seek to eliminate it?

Clearly it would be absurd to suggest its elimination in those societies in which rights are apportioned directly or indirectly on a racial basis. One could not deracialize South African society, for example, without it ceasing to be South African society, because rights to the franchise, to jobs, to education and to housing are allocated there on a racial basis. The myth is that rights are given equally but separately to Coloureds and Indians, and that Blacks are only treated differently because they are immigrants from the Homelands. In fact, separate facilities are, as the Brown versus the Board of Education judgment argued, inherently unequal, and the classification of Blacks as immigrants is a massive act of indirect discrimination.

The same kind of indirect discrimination, of course, exists in any society which classifies a part of its working population as 'guestworkers', as is the case in Western Germany, and so far as that part of the population is concerned government policies are racialist.

What can happen in such societies is the punishment of acts of aggression, including verbal acts of aggression, against minorities. This is the first and most elementary development of policy in a society which wishes to deracialize itself.

Coming back to the question of why any society should wish to deracialize itself, however, all that can be said is that there are societies which are so committed. The United States is one, so is post-revolutionary France and so in a different way is the Soviet

Union. The Constitution of the United States formally commits that country to equality of opportunity regardless of race; the French Revolution was fought on the basis of the slogan 'Liberty, Equality, and Fraternity'; and in the Soviet Union a revolutionary government exists which is committed to the Dictatorship of the Proletariat (not the White Proletariat or part of the Proletariat).

The situation in Britain is somewhat different. There is no written constitution and before 1948 all those who lived in the British Empire were British protected persons. What had to be worked out after that date was what rights British subjects migrating to the metropolis were to have as compared with the metropolitan population. In approaching this question, each of the political parties paid formal allegiance to a universalist ideology, the Conservatives to the notion of equality amongst the Queen's subjects, the Liberal Party to equality before the law and the Labour Party to the brotherhood of man.

One can with some justification be cynical about the extent to which these universalist ideologies actually influenced behaviour, and I have shown how, in the British case, ideologists gave way to doctrines of expediency in all cases (see Rex and Tomlinson 1979). Nonetheless, it is a sociological fact that such ideologies exist and that an argument can be held in all such societies against the continuance of racialist practice. It may even be that such developments are to be expected in any modern industrial society. If this is the case, then the arguments we have been discussing in this chapter are to be seen not as moral arguments in the abstract but as part of the factual social process.

The very first implications of such arguments is that ethnic populations should be protected against physical attack and derogatory abuse. This will in large part depend upon the behaviour of the police and the media. So far as the police are concerned they cannot be a law unto themselves. They must not harass any section of the population and they must give due protection to all sections of the population. These things will only occur if the policing policy of the society is governed by its overall political objectives, but such a situation is difficult to achieve since the police are employed to exercize legitimate force and the control of the use of that force is a subtle and taxing task.

With regard to derogatory abuse, it is necessary that a law against group libel should be rigorously enforced and the media themselves would have to be subject to a code of practice. These things again are difficult to achieve when the media are not subject to government control. What is wanted, however, is a situation in which there is a sufficient impetus for anti-racism for it to be

natural for a free press and free broadcasting to express such sentiments, rather than, as is often the case, more popular newspapers
and programmes allowing themselves to be used to foster
authoritarianism and anti-minority sentiment.

The next radical task must be the reform of language. This is
necessary because language always carries the legacy of the past,
and the language in use would not necessarily be adapted to anti-
racism. The renewal of language would be a prime task of racial
awareness training. On the other hand, it should be recognized that
language cannot be deracialized *in vacuo*. Its reform must go along
with a simultaneous reform of racialist practices. Unless it does, the
proposed new linguistic usage will be as artificial and irrelevant as
Sunday School lessons often are to normal healthy children.

The most crucial aspect of a deracializing policy, however, will
lie in the elimination of discriminatory practices. The debate about
positive discrimination is often misleading about this. It seems to
be saying that there is no actual discrimination and the minorities
are still behind. Therefore, it is argued, they must be given extra
rights. If positive discrimination is not to produce a backlash, it
must not appear in this light. It is necessary that positive action
should be taken to prevent discrimination in the first place, and if
this is unsuccessful, its consequences must be corrected. Policies on
these lines would give no moral justification for a backlash.

Finally, there is the question of breaking Myrdal's vicious cumulative cycle through the provision of new role-models. There is no
doubt that a cumulation cycle of this kind does operate. What
should be questioned, however, is the notion that the provision of
role-models can be achieved by the desparate means of promoting
the unqualified and the incompetent. What can be done, if it is
shown that there are insufficient minority representatives through
the monitoring of percentages attaining or employed at different
levels, is to provide training to ensure that *qualified* minority candidates are available. That may, in turn, imply pushing the process
further back to ensure that sufficient minority candidates emerge
from the schools of qualification. A qualified majority candidate
cannot have a grievance at a delay in his appointment if his
qualification was gained without fair competition from minority
people.

Conclusion

Racist thinking and racialist practice are a natural part of advanced
industrial societies and they are difficult to eliminate. Many of the

proposals for eliminating them are all too facile and the policies to which they lead are likely to be forced and to lead to a backlash. Nonetheless, there are universalistic elements in the political culture of all such societies and it is reasonable that systematic anti-racist and anti-racialist policies should be argued for. Despite present failures, there is at least some reason to suppose that in the long run they will be carried through, particularly when the minorities themselves find ways of exercizing political power.

In the long run, the guarantee of anti-racist policies will, in fact, depend upon the political power of the minorities, but even before them it is possible to envisage a society becoming committed to anti-racism. It can only do this, however, if such policies are backed unambiguously by the highest political authority. It is when there is doubt about commitment at the top that all of the policies which we have discussed here are put in jeopardy.

Chapter 7

The Concept of a Multi-Cultural Society

Four Types of Society

The previous chapter dealt with the concepts of racism and racialism. Racism involved belief systems which suggested that a category of individuals was for some sort of deterministic reason (usually biological) incapable of moving from one social position to another. Racialism referred to policies designed to prevent such movement. Racism referred to theory, racialism to practice. The confusing concept of institutional racism, however, was seen to refer to institutional policies which, without the support of racist theory of intent, produced unequal consequences for members of different racial categories. Additionally, it has to be recognized that the mere assertion of derogatory racial stereotypes involves a kind of action and is, therefore, hard to classify simply as either racism or racialism.

Racism or racialism in any of these forms is a matter of criticism or even of note only in a society committed to certain moral and political principles. These would include (a) the notion that whatever racial or ethnic category they may be in, human beings as such are in some sense entitled to equal treatment (b) that members of an ethnic or racial category should be protected from derogatory stereotyping and abuse (c) that, whatever inequalities of reward and outcome the society allows, any individual should have equality of opportunity in attaining these rewards or achieving these outcomes regardless of his or her race or ethnicity. In a word, racism and racialism are noted and criticized in a society in which a central ideal is that of equality or opportunity.

There is, however, another set of values involved in multi-racial and multi-cultural societies which conflicts with the notion of equality of opportunity. This set of values asserts that equality of opportunity involves cultural assimilation and the disappearance of all that is valued in the culture of all groups in a society other than the dominant one. Accordingly, it leads to the argument that something has to be done to ensure the survival of a plurality of cultures. A fundamental human right, it is sometimes said, is the right to be culturally different.

Unfortunately, the right to be different can all too readily be conceded without allowing for equality of opportunity and perhaps positively reinforcing inequality of opportunity. The existence of cultural difference can, as we saw when discussing ethnic boundaries, become a marker of the boundary between those who are accorded and those who are not accorded social, legal or political rights. The very concept of the plural society as it is used by Furnivall and M. G. Smith involves the recognition of cultural difference together with political or economic exploitation of one group by another and may lead to *de jure* or *de facto* differential incorporation. And, finally, it is clear that regimes like that in South Africa involving both racist theory and racialist practice not merely concede but positively insist upon the recognition of cultural differences.

How then is it possible to ensure both equality of opportunity and the toleration or encouragement of cultural difference? To answer this question we should ask whether it is not possible that the two ideals apply to different spheres of life. Is it, for example, possible that the notion of equality of opportunity is something that applies to the public domain and the ideal of multi-culturalism to the private domain?

If this distinction between the public and the private domain is allowed, then there could be four types of society as follows:

(a) Equality of opportunity in the public domain with multi-culturalism in the private domain

(b) Equality of opportunity in the public domain with mono-culturalism in the private domain

(c) Inequality of opportunity (between ethnic and racial groups) in the public domain with multi-culturalism in the private domain

(d) Inequality of opportunity (between ethnic and racial groups) with mono-culturalism in the private domain.

(a) would appear to represent the ideal for which many individuals are compaigning when they speak of a multi-cultural ideal.

Under this option, every individual would have equal rights before the law, in politics and in the market place as well as equality of social rights where these are provided by a welfare state, while at the same time having the right to conduct 'private' matters (i.e. religion, family arrangements, language and the cultural arts) according to the custom of a separate ethnic (sometimes racial) community.

(b) represents the formal ideal of the French Government in dealing with its minorities. The ideals of liberty and equality deriving from the French Revolution suggest a public domain marked by equal rights (of opportunity if not of outcomes) for all, and a cultural policy towards minorities which insists that they too are French and that they should assimilate to French cultural practices.

(c) is represented by the Apartheid state in South Africa. There the different racial groups are unequal estates differentially incorporated into the state, while the official ideology insists that the groups each have their own distinctive culture. The cultural separateness of the various groups is, indeed, said to have Divine support according to the theorists of what is called Christian National Education.

(d) is at least partially represented by the United States. Although since emancipation all groups have had equality before the law and in politics *de jure*, there has in fact been *de facto* inequality both in legal and political rights and in economic and social matters. Slavery, however, meant the elimination of separate cultural institutions amongst the Blacks and, although an unequal estate, they share the culture of White America. As against this it may, of course, be pointed out that Civil Rights Programmes have helped to achieve a measure of *de facto* equality for Blacks while at the same time a culture of Black Consciousness and Black Pride has promoted Black cultural difference.

The Separation of the Public and Private Domains

This classification of societies in terms of the way in which they deal with the public and the private domain, however, assumes that the distinction between the two domains can be readily drawn. Unfortunately, the distinction is very difficult to draw either theoretically or empirically. Most sociological theories point to the interdependence of the activities which we are seeking to confine to separate domains, and a number of institutions manifestly operate in both the private and the public sphere.

Any functionalist theory posits the interdependence of various functional sub-systems. A theory of the anthropological kind such as Malinowski's suggests that there are institutions of a primary sort which satisfy basic needs, and that the secondary and tertiary institutions (polity, economy, legal and political systems with the ultimate value system on the tertiary level) have the function of sustaining the basic ones as well as each other. There is no possibility of separating out two domains here, as though what went on in one did not depend upon and affect what went on in the other.

Even if it is argued that Malinowski's type of functionalism applies only to simple societies where all institutional activities are contained within families and kin-groups, it has to be noted that Parsons and others (Parsons 1952, Levy 1952) have suggested on a more abstract level that all societies at all stages of development have to make arrangements for dealing with the four functional problems which Parsons calls goal attainment, adaptation, intergration and latency or pattern maintenance and tension management. Thus the functioning of the policy (goal attainment system) and the economy (adaptative system) requires the functioning of the integrative system (having to do with law and morals) and the pattern maintenance and tension management system (in the family and community and in religion).

Functionalist theory would seem, therefore, at first sight to deny the possibility of the ideal multi-cultural society suggested by (a) above. On the other hand, plural society theory appears to insist that the separation of the moral and cultural order from the market place and the political order must mean that the latter are not governed by any 'common will'. The plural society would appear to be by definition one which departs from the peaceful ideals of multi-cultural ideology.

The actual history of European social institutions, however, suggests a more optimistic answer. The polity, the economy and the legal system have, it is true, been liberated from communal values, but they have developed their own more abstract values. On the other hand, it has seemed possible to permit the continuance of folk values and folk religion as long as these do not interfere with the functioning of the main political, economic and legal institutions of the society.

A great deal of mainstream sociological theory deals with the evolution of the new abstract value systems which a large-scale society requires. Tonnies saw that community must give way to association or society (1967). Durkheim wrote about organic solidarity based upon the division of labour which would replace the mechanical solidarity of small-scale community based on kinship (1974), and, even more radically, of an 'egoistic' society in which values were located in the minds of separate and separated individuals (1952). Finally, Weber saw in the Calvinist religion the end-point of an increasingly rationalistic trend in religion (1930) and together with that the development of political leadership based upon rational legal authority (Weber 1968).

Moral and legal systems of an abstract character were seen then as governing the social evolution of the modern state and of a formally rational capitalist economy. That was why the 'problem of order' to which Parsons refers (1937) was solved and why Western societies did not degenerate into a war of all against all: Furnivall, moreover, was quite right to note that in colonial society the institutions of the market place developed, but *without* the common will which had characterized them in Europe.

The development of an abstract public morality, law and religion, however, by no means implied the disappearance of folk morality, folk culture and folk religion. These now came to fulfil new functions. On the one hand, they bound men together into separate communities into which individuals were socialized and within which they achieved their own identities. On the other, they provided for what Parsons called Pattern Maintenance and Tension Management. Living in the larger world with its abstract moral principles was, so Parsons believed, only psychologically possible if individuals also had the possibility of a retreat where they could enjoy more intimate relations and 'let their hair down'.

The ideal of the multi-cultural society outlined in (a) above really presupposes the evolution of the modern type of society about which Wener and Durkheim especially wrote. In simple societies, full morality and kinship structures had to govern the full range of human activity. In an abstract and impersonal society, a new, more abstract form of law and morality had to be developed to govern large-scale political and economic organizations, while the old folk culture and morality helped the individual to retain some sort of psychological stability, through more immediate social interdependence.

The first of the institutions which constitute the public domain are those of law, politics and the economy. So far as law is concerned this determines the rights of any individual and the way in which he is incorporated into the society. The very mark of the plural society was that different categories were differentially incorporated. In the ideal society (a), on the other hand, we are positing that all individuals are equally incorporated and that they have equality before the courts. In the sphere of politics, again in the plural society different groups have different degrees of political power. In the ideal society, each individual is deemed to have the right to the same amount of political power, whether through the vote or by other means. Actual political outcomes depend upon the contests and conflicts which go on between individuals thus possessed of power.

The economy refers in the first place to the institution of the market. As a mode of organization this rests as we have seen upon the use of a particular kind of sanction, namely 'going to another supplier'. It excludes the use of force. It also, however, excludes the concept of charity. Charity is a concept which belongs to the world of the community and folk morality. What is involved here is the more abstract morality or sticking to the rules of the game which apply to markets (Furnivall's common will).

We should also note that what we call the economy here might be replaced by another type of allocative system or what is sometimes called a command economy. Here certain abstract goals are made explicit and organizations are set up to achieve them. But the best that such a system can achieve is formal justice. There is no principle of charity, which is again assigned to the folk community.

Of course, the world of abstract macro-institutions is not simple and peaceful. The pursuit of directly political goals involves conflict, and markets break down and give way to collective bargaining and political conflict. What we are pointing out here is that the ideal society (a) is simply one in which no individual has more or less rights or a greater or lesser capacity to operate in this world because of his or her ethnic category.

One of the difficulties which emerges from the pursuit of an ideal called a multi-cultural society, however, is that it is sometimes suggested that individuals should receive different treatment in the public domain. It cannot be pointed out too strongly that if this were the case we would move towards the plural society in Furnivall's and Smith's sense of the term, and that this would involve differential incorporation of groups into a society at least *de facto* if not *de jure*. At best it would involve a sort of paternalism towards the minority group. Other people would have their needs provided for by separate functional departments of government and the economy, but the needs of the minority would be provided by a special Department of Minority Affairs. This *is* too often the outcome when minority members campaign for special treatment. What they get is differential incorporation.

There are some societies in the world where different racial or ethnic groups contest the control of the institutions of the public sphere and reach a compromise in which they share control. Thus, for example, Walloons and Flemish contest control of the Belgian state and economy. Quebecois and Anglo-Canadians contest the control of Quebec, and amongst White South Africans control is contested between English and Afrikaans speakers. Such contests are resolved by agreeing sets of rules about such matters as entry to the Civil Service or about the languages to be used by that Civil Service. Often this implies monitored equal access for the contesting groups, but one other possibility common in the world is that while one group assumes command of government the other assumes command of the economy.

All such cases, however, are examples of the plural society. They do not come under the heading (a) above and are not what is meant by those who campaign for a multi-cultural society. In Britain, for instance, there is today an Indian, Pakistani and Bangladeshi minority which argues for multi-culturalism. No one suggests, however, that this means a right of the groups as such to a share in the control of government or that the various languages concerned should become Civil Service languages. What is sought is equality of opportunity in these spheres, together with a respect for their right to manage their own domestic and communal affairs in their own way. This is all that is usually claimed under the banner of multi-culturalism.

The boundaries of the public domain

So far we have discussed the institutions of law, politics and the economy as institutions of the public domain. The state, however, also intervenes in matters which we have so far suggested belong to the private domain. It may seek to encourage not merely efficient production in the economic sphere, but a way of running the economy so that it guarantees full employment to the whole population. It may seek to protect job security by allowing trades unions to engage in collective bargaining and in other ways. It may make provision through social insurance so that individuals without employment still have an income. It may build houses and let them or subsidize the building of houses for private ownership. It may provide education for children and for adults, and it may provide social work services to help in resolving personal and family problems. It is this set of provisions and equivalent rights that we referred to in an earlier chapter as 'the Welfare State deal', and which leads T. H. Marshall (1950) to say that it is a mark of the modern state that it provides, in addition to legal and political rights, a substantial body of social rights. So much is this the case that Marshall argues that the worker today has a greater sense of loyalty to the state and the nation than he does to his class. In the terms of this chapter, he might have added that primary loyalty is now to the public domain, with the institutions of the private domain possibly shrinking to insignificance.

Undoubtedly, functions have been lost by the family and community to the state, although there is an argument that state intervention actually supports the family and enables it to perform its primary tasks of consumption and socialization more effectively (Fletcher 1957). But, in any case, this is something which on the whole individuals accept. A degree of state provision for family welfare seems inevitable in the modern world. Perhaps of greater significance, however, is that some of the activities of the state do appear to infringe on the sphere of the family and community. This is particularly true of education and social welfare.

A modern educational system has three clear functions. It selects individuals on the basis of their achievement for training and eventual acceptance into various occupational roles. It transmits important skills necessary for survival and for work in industry. But it also transmits moral values. This third function brings it into conflict with the private domain, for one part of the socialization process consists precisely in the transmission of moral values.

Clearly no ethnic minority objects to the existence of a selective mechanism being part of the public domain. What is important is simply that this mechanism should give equal opportunity to all. Again, if the minority is committed to living by employment in the industrial system, it will itself wish to take advantage of any skill training which is available. Moral training, however, involves other issues.

Insofar as it is simply concerned with the transmission of what might be called the civic morality and culture, the problems raised by moral training through the schools will be small. (By civic morality here, I mean the set of values of an abstract kind which Weber and Durkheim believed were essential to the operation of a modern society.) True, there will be doubts about the desirability of encouraging competition and individualist attitudes because, taken out of context, these conflict with the principles of charity and mutual and underlying local communities and the private domain. But this is an inherent tension in an industrial society with which industrial man has learned to live. Moreover, parts of this civic morality are of value and importance to minorities. This is especially true of the notion of equality of opportunity. Much more important than any objection to this aspect of the school's moral role is the objection to its interference in matters which are thought of as private or as involving individual choice. This is true of all matters relating to sex, marriage, the family and religion.

It is arguable that schools ought not to intervene in these matters at all or to do so only on the most general and basic level. Such an argument turns upon showing that a variety of practices in these spheres in no way prevents the proper functioning of the institution of state and society and may positively assist it. The counter-argument is that it is of concern to the state how family matters are arranged, both because the state is concerned with the law of inheritance and because it has to uphold individual rights even against the family.

On family matters, there are considerable tensions between minority communities and the school in contemporary Britain. Amongst Indians, for example, there is great emphasis upon arranged marriages and upon the relative seclusion and modesty of females. Neither the official curriculum of British schools nor the peer group culture, in which minority children inevitably partici-pate, fosters the relevant values. The schools may be quite unneces-sarily provocative, as when some of them require participation of girls in mixed swimming classes, but, more generally, the whole ethos of the school, based as it is on the encouragement of indi-vidual choice and free competition, strikes at the root of any tight-knit marriage and family system.

There is often a fundamental clash of values on these matters in any modern society. The notion of equality of opportunity appears to point to the rights not simply of families but to those of all individuals, male and female, if necessary against the constraints imposed by families. Feminism has made the issues here especially sharp. It is unacceptable in terms of feminist values that a woman should be forced into a marriage to which she does not freely assent, and equally unacceptable that girls should be denied the maximum degree of education of which they are capable because of some preconceived community notion of the female role.

Such emphases in the argument are, from the point of view of many Indian parents, quite misleading. They fail to take note of the fact that an arranged marriage reflects the care which a family shows towards its daughters, guaranteeing them a dowry far more substantial than anything which an English girl might get from her parents. Indeed, it can be said that the whole system gives the bride more rights against her husband that does the notion of marriage based on random selection and romantic love. Much more than this, however, the assertion of freedom in the sexual sphere is bound up with a whole set of values about the marketability of sex which is reflected in the media and in sex shops. The feminist demand for greater freedom is seen as part of this larger package and it is this larger package which offends against all Indian con-cepts of modesty and love.

There is no point in seeking to resolve this clash of values here. It is simply important to know that it exists and that in a society which seeks to achieve both equality of opportunity and the toleration of cultural diversity, institutional arrangements will evolve to deal with the tension. In the case mentioned, parents will be very positively identified with what the school has to offer by way of increasing equality of opportunity, but may seek to limit its role by the withdrawal of their children from certain kinds of activity and also by seeking to provide supplementary moral education outside the school.

Another potential source of discord is religion. Here, however, the way has been prepared in a Christian society for dealing with potential conflicts. Because the various Christian sects and denominations had engaged in conflicts, wars and civil wars which threatened the unity of the state, most nominally Christian societies had already downgraded religion to a matter of minor importance towards which there was no danger in exercizing toleration. Once, therefore, Roman Catholics were given the right to teach their own religion in schools, there was no barrier in principle to allowing Islam or Sikhism or Hinduism to be taught in a similar way. Rather more problematic, however, were those religions and quasi-religions like Ras-Tafarianism which had strong political overtones.

Wider than the religious question was that of instruction in minority cultures, thought by many to be the key issue in any programme of multi-cultural education. Such innovations, however, were far from popular with minority communities, who saw them as diverting time and energies from subjects more important for examination success and, in any case, as caricatures of their culture. The strong preference was that, unless such teaching could be carried out in schools by minority teachers, it was best done outside school hours.

Language created greater dilemmas. Teaching in mother tongues and teaching of mother tongues have both been seen to be important by a wide variety of minority communities. Teaching *in* the mother tongue is important at the outset for those who do not speak the main school language. If they are simply confronted by this other language on entering school, children's education is likely to be seriously retarded. Initial teaching in the mother tongue is required, therefore, with the main language gradually introduced until it finally replaces mother tongues as the medium of instruction. Paradoxically, the importance of using mother tongue as an initial medium of instruction is that it can facilitate assimilation.

The teaching *of* mother tongue is of separate importance. Systematic provision of such teaching is beyond the means of most minority communities, and if it is literally left to mothers it will simply become a restricted ghetto language. Many minority people want to have financial support for the maintenance of mother tongue, so that it can be used to enlarge the cultural experience of the group. It cannot, in the kind of society we have in mind, even attain anything like the equality which a language might acquire with the main language in a bilingual state. But there is no reason why minority people should not be able to express themselves and communicate with each other about their experiences in their own language.

It is being suggested here that once we recognize the inherent tensions to be found in the educational system because it is at once part of the public and the private domain, it is possible to produce a balance of control. The school should be concerned with selection, with the transmission of skills and with the inculcation of what we have called the civic morality. The community should control education in all matters having to do with their own language, with religion and family affairs. It is certainly a possibility that the state might legitimately be called upon to provide financial support for such activity.

The other alternative is to take education out of the public domain and make it an intra-communal matter. This has been done in England in the case of church schools and, in principle, no new ground would be broken if, say, Muslim or Hindu schools received a similar recognition. Obviously, a danger in such schools would be that the tasks fulfilled by mainstream schools would be subordinated to inculcation of communal values, but a balance could be struck here in which the controllers of the minority schools themselves recognized the instrumental value of education in a modern society along with education in their own culture. In fact, if there were this recognition, it might be more possible to achieve the right balance in a school controlled by the minority than in normal majority schools which found themselves in tension with minority cultures.

Clearly education is one sphere, however, in which the distinction between that which is necessary for a large-scale secular society and that which is necessary from the point of view of maintaining the culture and tradition of a minority community is most difficult to draw. Another even more difficult area is in connection with social welfare and social work. In such circumstances social workers claim that what is necessary in dealing with minorities is a special kind of multi-cultural social work. If, however, the problems of minority people are so different, would it not be possible for the community itself to be subsidized so that it could take care of its

own? Alternatively, is the problem not that of combining professional standards with sensitivity to community values? In that case,
would not the answer be to train social workers from the communities so that they can add professionalism to their existing
sensitivity? The problems of trying to train majority social workers
in sensitivity is much more difficult than that of training already
sensitive minority people in professional standards.

Racism in dealing with the private domain

One recurrent problem in all thinking about a multi-cultural society
is that, although there is a case for recognizing differences and
trying to make apppropriate differential provision for those who
are culturally different, there is always the danger that what might
be provided would be of inferior quality. This is one way in which
racist theory and racialist practice intrudes into minority policy.
The advocacy of multi-culturalism can itself be a form of racism.
'They are different,' the argument runs, 'therefore they cannot be
expected to have the same provisions as us. It would do them no
good.' Certainly this attitude towards multi-culturalism is not
compatible with a policy of equality of opportunity.

What may be at stake here is whether the minority community
obtains equal incorporation into the society or *de facto* differential
incorporation. Very often those who advocate multi-culturalism
are proposing the latter.

But equally, racism can often lie behind opposition to multi-
culturalism. The notion that minority cultures involve reactionary
elements may be used to conceal this. There is an argument, for
instance, that arranged marriage restricts the freedom of minority
women and that it is an affront to feminist standards. When,
however, arranged marriage is given prominence before all else in
an account of minority culture, and is seen only from a partial
point of view, we may suspect that the critic is hostile to the minority culture and is using the argument about arranged marriage as
a form of derogatory abuse.

The boundaries of the private domain

The nature of the sociological problem with which we now have to
deal is this. For a member of the majority in a society, the world
of the family and the primary community is an integrated structural
part of the whole network of social relations which constitutes his
or her society. It is also a functional sub-system of the whole and
its culture is continuous with that of the main society. Amongst
ethnic minorities, the situation is wholly different. For such
minorities, the family and community are part of another social

system and another culture. Quite possibly, the extended kinship group in that society carried much more weight than it does in an industrial society, and in some cases provided the whole of the social structure. This kinship group is now fractured by a process of migration and has a new and modified structure. In part, this structure and the culture which it bears cannot fit with and be integrated into the society of settlement, but, after a while, the latter's structure and culture are assumed as the minority family and community structure is assigned a role and a function within an alien social system which surrounds it.

What we are assuming here, of course, are politically weak immigrant minorities. The alternative situations would be those in which ethnically or racially distinguishable minorities lived in some measure structurally separated from one another, but having to enter into relations with each other in the public arena, and the situation in a colonial territory where the structure of the public arena was created by a powerful immigrant minority, and other groups whether native-born or immigrant had to operate within it. However, we are considering what would have to be done to create a multi-cultural society with equal opportunity and since this ideal is a highly unrealistic one in the other two cases, we are justified in concentrating on the question of what would be involved in creating such a society where there are immigrant minorities.

The first thing to notice about the primary community structure amongst such immigrant minorities is that it plays a larger part in the life of its members than does any such structure amongst the minority. Tonnies' observation that specialized associations succeed communities historically is true as a generalization about isolated societies engaged in a unilinear evolution. But in some measure, community always survives at local level and it survives much more strongly amongst immigrant minorities than it does elsewhere.

Perhaps the most important function of the immigrant minority community is primary socialization. In the case of the majority, this function is performed by the family and the family exists in relative isolation from a larger community or network. The family is also likely to be central in the primary socialization of a member of the immigrant community, but it is in any case not so isolated from larger kinship structures as is the majority family, and because there is always the likelihood that families themselves will be split up by migration, substitutes have often to be found to fill key roles. In terms of immediate personal contacts, therefore, the socializing community which surrounds any individual is larger, and more people are involved in his or her socialization.

The family and the wider kin-groups, however, are not solely

socializing agencies. They also form units for economic mobilization, and this function may be performed even when the members are separated from each other by migration. The family and
kin-group have an estate to which members may be expected to
contribute, either in terms of property or in terms of skills and
qualifications. An event like marriage, therefore, is not and cannot
be solely a matter of individual choice. It involves the transfer of
capital from one group to another and as a result the linking of two
groups. At the same time, the new family constituted by marriage
starts with a carefully husbanded inheritance of material and social
capital.

Because extended kinship is seriously damaged by the fact of
migration, the networks within which family life occurs come to
depend more upon artificial structures, which are thought of as
associations but which are actually social structures through which
the wider community life is expressed. As I have suggested in
Chapter 4 and at greater length elsewhere (Rex 1973), the functions
of these associations include acting as a kind of community trade
union and negotiating on its behalf with the larger society, over-
coming the social isolation of individuals, affirming beliefs and
values, and ministering to the needs of individuals and families
through various types of charitable and social work.

Of particular importance is the role of the associations in the
affirmation of beliefs and values. Included in this role is the
offering of beliefs to the individual about himself, that is to say
identity options or ideas as to who he or she is. Naturally it is not
the case that individuals automatically accept these options, but the
associations are flexible instruments through which new identities
appropriate to the new situation are suggested as possible.

The whole primary community of the ethnic minority, including
its associations, has a function in relation to the larger society. It
is the function which Parsons chooses to call pattern maitenance
and tension management but, sociological jargon aside, we may say
that it provides the individual with a concept of who he is as he
embarks on action in the outside world, and it also gives him moral
and material support in coping with the exigencies of his existence.
To the extent that it performs these functions, the ethnic immigrant
community becomes a functioning part of the larger society,
whatever the particular form of its social structure and whatever
the content of its culture. This is why the idea of a multi-cultural
society is supported to the extent that it is. In crude Marxist terminology it may be said to provide the essential social machinery for
the reproduction of the labour force.

Another feature of the minority communities is that they have religions different from that of the society of settlement. These religions were often evolved as world religions and offer ideas about man's relation to nature and to his fellow-man which go far beyond the present situation. As such they cannot be simply functional. Yet, whatever their particular content, they do provide a dogmatic and metaphysical underpinning for all beliefs and, therefore, help to promote the psychological security which the whole community structure gives. Religious congregations, moreover, provide profound secondary reinforcement to other structures of kin and community.

Ethnic immigrant community culture, however, stands for far more than just these functions. It provides, at least potentially, a basis for dealing with the whole world of social relations and is a competitor with the main culture of the society in offering its interpretation of these. The question has to be asked, therefore, whether one could envisage a multi-cultural society in which all cultures were taken equally seriously. Is it simply because we only think about them as generalized community structures with definite and restricted functions that we tolerate the idea of multi-culturalism at all?

One way of looking at this matter, however, does suggest that a kind of multi-culturalism is possible. This is if we look on the secular civic culture as a common and necessary component of all cultures in advanced industrial societies. This secular civic culture involves the set of beliefs about which Weber and Durkheim wrote, that is to say a highly rationalistic and limited set of beliefs. All other aspects of all cultures are downgraded in their importance, including the regional folk and even class cultures of the majority. From the point of view of the minority community, the civic culture includes the right of all individuals to equality of opportunity as well as other legal and political rights, and its own culture can readily be adapted to these ideas. In fact, the possibility of different cultures coexisting depends upon them all accepting this shared and common set of ideas. Multi-culturalism is only likely to be tolerated if it does not threaten the shared civic culture including, of course, the idea of equality of opportunity. Not surprisingly, therefore, the notion of multi-culturalism comes to mean for the minorities anti-racism, which asserts that no individual should be denied opportunity because of his race, ethnicity, or culture. This is the way in which arguments about multi-cultural education have always developed. The reason why the term multi-cultural is often retained, however, is that in an ideal multi-cultural society all cultures come to share a common core which prevents the derogation of anyone because of his cultural background.

The feasibility and limits of multi-culturalism
Multi-culturalism, then, is a feasible social and political ideal. The real difficulty is that what may gain support under this title will be a fraudulent alternative which dissociates multi-culturalism from equality of opportunity and thereby opens the way to *de facto* differential incorporation.

One further question may be asked, however. This is whether there will ever be a society which becomes and remains multi-cultural. The case of Indians in Britain is something of a test case. They clearly will not be assimilated over three or four generations as have the Irish in Britain or Southern Europeans in N.W. Europe or the United States. They also have a long historically-based culture rooted in several of the great world religions. Yet it is also the case that their children, attending British schools, learning the civic culture and sharing the interests of their British peers, will find increasingly that they are drawn towards assimilation. In the second generation which has now reached adulthood, there is already an uneasy compromise between participation in an adult and teenage world on terms of equality and respect with British adults and teenagers, and living in an ethnic minority world. It also seems possible that, as there are more and more examples of success by Indians, some of the remaining racism and racialism which is directed towards them will disappear. In these circumstances, there will soon be a generation for whom the multi-cultural ideal is not at all appealing. In those circumstances, insistence upon it can only involve a form of racism, of forcing a category of individuals into a lifestyle which they do not want.

It must, therefore, be said as a final point that the creation of a multi-cultural society must involve an element of voluntarism. Those who wish to assimilate should be allowed to do so. Those who prefer to retain their separate culture should also be allowed to do that. Neither a forced process of multi-culturalism nor a forced process of assimilation is acceptable. We are dealing with one stage in the history of majority-minority relations and the important point is to create the kind of society in which all people may choose their cultural affiliations. In the case of Indians, some will choose assimilation, some will attempt to retain their culture and social organization in the land of settlement, others will retain them with a view to being equipped to live in the international Diaspora.

In these two final chapters, we have moved away from discussing what structures exist to discussing those which might be desirable. This is not because we are confusing an 'ought' with an 'is'. Social science cannot tell us what we should do. What it can do, however,

is examine ideals to see whether they are confused and contradict-
ory and to spell them out in versions which are feasible. It is to be
hoped that this book as a whole, setting out a range of actual and
ideal forms of race and ethnic relations, will contribute to this end.

Bibliography

Adorno, Theodor, *et al.* (1950) *The Authoritarian Personality.* Harper and Row, New York.

Banton, Michael (1969) *Race relations.* Tavistock, London.

Banton, Michael (1970) 'The Idea of Race' in Zubaida, Sami (Ed) (1970), *Race and Racialism.* Tavistock, London.

Banton, Michael (1983) *Racial and Ethnic Competition.* Cambridge University Press.

Barth, Frederick (1959) *Political Leadership among the Swat Pathans.* London School of Economics Monographs on Social Anthropology, No. 19, London.

Barth, Frederick (1969) *Ethnic Groups and Boundaries.* Allen and Unwin, London.

Berger, Peter, and Luckmann, Thomas (1967) *The Social Construction of Reality.* Allen Lane, London.

Blau, Peter Michael (1964) *Exchange and Power in Social Life.* Wiley, New York.

Bonacich, Edna, (1973) 'A Theory of Middlemen Minorities', *American Sociological Review.* No. 38, New York.

Bonacich, Edna (1980) 'Class Approaches to Ethnicity and Race', *Insurgent Sociologist.* Vol. X, No. 2, New York.

Brenner, Robert (1979) 'The Origins of Capitalist Development—A Critique of Neo-Smithian Marxism', *New Left Review.* No. 104, London.

Carmichael, Stokely, and Hamilton, Charles V. (1968) *Black Power—The Politics of Liberation in America.* Cape, London.

Chase, Stuart (1938) *The Tyranny of Words.* Methuen, London.

Cohen, Abner, ed. (1974) *Urban Ethnicity.* Tavistock, London.

Cohen, Yehudi (1969) 'Social Boundary Systems', *Current Anthropology*. 10, London.

Cox, Oliver Cromwell (1970) *Caste, Class and Race*. Monthly Review Press, New York.

de Kiewiet (1948) *A History of South Africa—Social and Economic*. Oxford University Press, London.

Devereux, Edward C. (1961) 'Parsons' Sociological Theory' in *The Social Theories of Talcott Parsons*, ed. M. Black. Prentice Hill, New York.

Doeringer, Peter, and Piore, Michael (1971) *Internal Labour Markets and Manpower Analysis*. Health, Lexington, Massachusetts.

Dollard, John *et al.* (1939) *Frustration and Aggression*. Yale University Press.

Dollard, John (1957) *Caste and Class in a Southern Town*. Doubleday, New York.

Dummett, Ann (1973) *A Portrait of British Racism*. Penguin Books, Hammondsworth.

Durkheim, Emile (1915) *The Elementary Forms of Religious Life*. Allen and Unwin, London.

Durkheim, Emile (1938) *The Rules of Sociological Method*. Chicago University Press.

Durkheim, Emile (1952) *Suicide*. Routledge and Kegan Paul, London.

Durkheim, Emile (1974) *The Division of Labour in Society*. Free Press, Glencoe.

Ekeh, Peter (1979) *Social Exchange Theory—The Two Traditions*. Heinemann, London.

Elkins, Stanley (1959) *Slavery—A Problem in American Institutional and Intellectual Life*, Chicago University Press.

Fanon, Frantz (1952) *Black Skins, White Masks*

Fanon, Frantz (1965) *The Wretched of the Earth*. MacGibbon and Kee, London.

Fletcher, Ronald (1957) *The Family and Marriage in Britain—An Analysis and Moral Assessment*. Penguin Books, Harmondsworth.

Frank, Andre Gunder (1967) *Capitalism and Underdevelopment in Latin America*. Monthly Review Press, New York.

Freyre, Gilberto (1963) *The Mansions and the Shanties—The Making of Modern Brazil*. Alfred Knopf, New York.

Fromm, Eric (1942) The Fear of Freedom, Routledge and Kegan Paul, London.

Furnivall, John Sydenham (1939) *Netherlands India—A Study of Plural Economy*. Cambridge University Press.

Furnivall, John Sydenham (1968) *Colonial Policy and Practice*, Cambridge University Press.

Geertz, Clifford (1963) *Old Societies and New States—The Quest for Modernity in Asia and Africa*. Free Press, Glencoe.

Gordon, Milton M. (1978) *Human Nature, Class and Ethnicity*. Oxford University Press, New York.

Hall, Stuart (1980) 'Race Articulation and Societies Structured in Dominance' in UNESCO *Sociological Theories of Race and Colonialism*, UNESCO.

Hanke, Lewis (1959) *Aristotle and the American Indians—A Study in Race Prejudice in the Modern World*. Hollis and Carter, New York.

Hechter, Michael (1983) *The Micro Foundations of Macro Sociology*, Temple University Press, Philadelphia.

Hiernaux, Jean (1965) 'Introduction—The Moscow Expert Meeting', *International Social Science Journal*, Vol. XVII, No. 1, UNESCO, Paris.

Homans, George (1961) *Social Behaviour*. Harcourt Brace World, New York.

HMSO (1976) *Race Relations Act 1976*, Chapter 74.

HMSO (1977) *Policy for the Inner Cities*, Cmd 6845.

Jay, Martin (1973) *The Dialectical Imagination—A History of the Frankfurt School and the Institute of Social Research*, Heinemann, London.

Katz, Judy (1978) *White Awareness Handbook for Anti-Racist Training*, University of Oklahoma.

Levy, Marion (1952) *The Structure of Society*, Princeton University Press.

Lipset, Seymour Martin (1960) *Political Man*, Heinemann, London.

Lundberg, George (1939) *Foundations of Sociology*, MacMillan, New York.

Malinowski, Bronislaw (1944) *A Scientific Theory of Culture*, University of North Carolina Press, Chapel Hill.

Marshall, Thomas Humphrey (1950) *Citizenship and Social Class and Other Essays*, Cambridge University Press.

Marx, Karl (1957) 'Theses on Feuerbach' in Karl Marx and Frederick Engels *On Religion*, Foreign Languages Publishing House, Moscow.

Marx, Karl (1961) *Capital*, Foreign Languages Publishing House, Moscow.

Marx, Karl and Engels, Friderich (1962a) 'The Communist Manifesto' in *Karl Marx and Frederick Engels Selected Works*, Vol. 1, Foreign Languages Publishing House, Moscow.

Marx, Karl (1962b) 'Address to the Communist League' in *Karl Marx and Frederick Engels Selected Works*, Vol, 1, Foreign Languages Publishing House, Moscow.

Marx, Karl (1962c) 'Preface to the Critique of Political Economy' in *Karl Marx and Frederick Engels, Selected Works*, Vol. 1, Foreign Languages Publishing House, Moscow.

Marx, Karl (1962d) *The Poverty of Philosophy*, Foreign Languages Publishing House, Moscow.

Marx, Karl (1967) 'Toward the Critique of the Hegelian Philosophy of Law : Introduction' in Easton, Lloyd D., and Guddatt Kurt H., *Writings of the Young Marx on Philosophy and Society*, Anchor Books, New York.

Mason, David, and Rex, John, eds (1986) *Theories of Ethnic and Race Relations*, Cambridge University Press.

Montagu, Ashley (1972) *Statement on Race*, Oxford University Press.

Myrdal, Gunnar (1944) *An American Dilemma*, Harper Bros., New York.

Myrdal, Gunnar (1964) *Challenge to Affluence*, Macmillan, London.

National Committe for Commonwealth Immigrants (1967) *Areas of Special Housing Needs*, London.

Pareto, Vilfredo (1963) *The Mind and Society—A Treatise on Sociology*, 4 Vols., Dover Books.

Parsons, Talcott (1949) *The Structure of Social Action*, Free Press of Glencoe, Illinois.

Parsons, Talcott (1952) *The Social System*, Tavistock, London.

Parson, Talcott and Shils, Edward, eds. (1962) *Towards a General Theory of Action*, Harper and Row, New York.

Parsons, Talcott, Bales, Robert, and Shils, Edward (1953) *Working Papers in the Theory of Action*, Free Press of Glencoe, Illinois.

Rex, John (1961) *Key Problems of Sociological Theory*, Routledge and Kegan Paul, London.

Rex, John (1973) *Race Colonialism and the City*, Routledge and Kegan Paul, London.

Rex, John (1983) *Race Relations in Sociological Theory*, Weidenfeld and Nicolson, London 1970. Second revised edition, Routledge and Kegan Paul, London.

Rex, John (1985) 'Neo-Kantianism Methodological Individualism and Michael Banton' *Ethnic and Racial Studies*, Vol. 8, No. 3, Routledge and Kegan Paul, London.

Rex, John (1986) 'Race and Ethnicity' in *Introducing Sociology*, ed., P. Worsley. New edition, Penguin Books, Harmondsworth.

Rex, John, and Moore, Robert (1967) *Race, Community and Conflict*, Oxford University Press, London.

Rex, John, and Tomlinson, Sally (1979) *Colonial Immigrants in a British City*, Routledge and Kegan Paul, London.

Schelsky, Helmut (1957) *Soziologische Bemerkungen Zur Rolle der Schule in Unserer Gesellschefruer Fassung*. Unpublished paper quoted by Dahrendorf, Ralf, *Class and Class Conflict in Industrial Society*, Routledge and Kegan Paul, London.

Schermerhorn, Richard (1970) *Comparative Ethnic Relations—A Framework for Theory and Research*, Random House, New York.

Schutz, Alfred (1967) *The Phenomenology of the Social World*, North Western University Press.

Smith, David (1967) *Racial Disadvantage in Britain*, Penguin Books, Harmondsworth.

Smith, Michael Garfield (1965) 'The Plural Society in the British West Indies', University of California Press, Berkeley.

Smith, Michael Garfield and Kuper, Leo, eds. (1969) *Pluralism in Africa*, University of California Press, Berkeley.

Smith, Michael Garfield (1974) *Corporations and Society*, Duckworth, London.

Sorel, Georges (1961) *Reflections on Violence*, Collier-MacMillan, London.

Sumner, William Graham (1959) *Folkways*, Ginn, New York 1906, Dover Publications 1959.

Tinker, Hugh (1974) *A New System of Slavery—The Export of Indian Labour Overseas 1830-1920*, Oxford University Press.

Tonnies, Ferdinand (1967) *Community and Society*, Translated by Charles P. Loonis, Harper and Row, New York.

Van den Berghe, Pierre Louis (1978) *Race and Racism—A Comparative Perspective*, Wiley, New York.

Wallerstein, Immanuel (1974) *The Modern World System*, Academic Press, New York.

Wallman, Sandra, (1979) 'The Boundaries of Race. Processes of Ethnicity in England' in *Man*, No. 13, pp. 200-217.

Wallman, Sandra (1986) 'The Application of Anthropological Theory to the Study of Boundary Processes' in Mason, David, and Rex, John *Theories of Ethnic and Race Relations*, Cambridge University Press.

Warner, W. Lloyd (1936) 'American Class and Caste' in *American Journal of Sociology*, Vol. XLII, September, pp. 234-7.

Warner, William Lloyd and Lunt, Paul S. (1947) 'The Soccial System of a Modern Community', Yale University Press, New Haven, Connecticut.

Weber, Max (1930) *The Protestant Ethic and the Spirit of Capitalism*, George Allen and Unwin, London.

Weber, Max (1962) *General Economic History*, Collier Books, New York.

Weber, Max (1968) *Economy and Society*, 3 Volumes, Bedminster Press, New York.

Weber, Max (1976) *The Agrarian Sociology of Ancient Civilization*, New Left Books, London.

Wellman, David T. (1977) *Portraits of White Racism*, Cambridge University Press, London.

Index

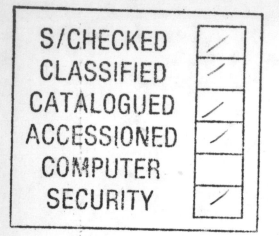